IMAGES
*of America*

# Detroit's Holy Family Church
## 100 Years of Sicilian Tradition

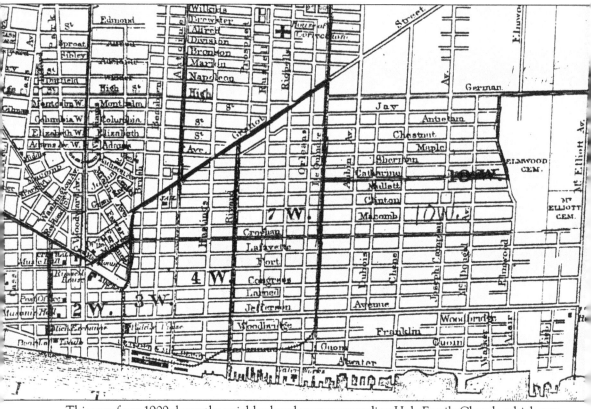

This map from 1909 shows the neighborhood once surrounding Holy Family Church, which was located on the corner of East Fort and Hastings Streets.

## IMAGES
### *of America*

# DETROIT'S HOLY FAMILY CHURCH
## 100 YEARS OF SICILIAN TRADITION

Bonnie Leone

ARCADIA
PUBLISHING

Published by Arcadia Publishing
Charleston SC, Chicago IL, Portsmouth NH, San Francisco CA


Library of Congress Catalog Card Number: 2007941897

For all general information contact Arcadia Publishing at: Telephone
843-853-2070
Fax 843-853-0044
E-mail sales@arcadiapublishing.com
For customer service and orders:
Toll-Free 1-888-313-2665

Visit us on the Internet at www.arcadiapublishing.com

*I dedicate this book to my mother, Margaret VanDerziel;*
*to my children Melissa Paalanen and Leo Leone;*
*to my husband, William Leone;*
*to those first Southern Italian and Sicilian immigrants;*
*and to their descendants.*

# CONTENTS

# ACKNOWLEDGMENTS

First thanks go to Sam DiMaggio and Angie (Maniacci) DiMaggio, who a decade ago asked my now-husband, William Leone, to bring me to the church that his grandparents, Vito Leone and Provvidenza Pagano, once belonged to on the feast day of Madonna delle Grazie, so that they might meet me. They introduced me to the tradition of the Latin mass, Italian feast days, and a church rich in beauty and history; because of this I never left Sacra Famiglia and I wrote this book.

Throughout the last year I have spent countless hours tracing families, collecting records, and going through photographs. My gratitude goes out to all of the wonderful people to whom I will never be able to thank enough for their time, help, and photographs (or all of the above) so that I may preserve the first 100 years of Sacra Famiglia in a book. Mucho grande thanks go to Josephine DeMaria, Jack Tocco, Peter and Grace Tocco, Joe D'Anna, Joe Biondo, Vito Manzella, Bill Bagnasco, Joe Maniacci, Rose Patchett, Joe Donofrio, Fr. Lawrence Fares, Frank and Josephine Carta, Rosary Amore, Josephine Biundo, Salvatore Ciaramitaro, Doris Fanfalone, Maria Sugameli, Sandra Smith, Debbie Patterson, Maria Rosati, Grace Corrollo, Al Chirco, Elizabeth Falsone, Tony Maisano, Helen Brennan, Joe Mazzola, Rose Marie Fessler, Gina Mangiapane, Sara Scrivano, Fran Marie Silveria, Andrea and Antoniatta Pacitto, Joe and Rose Amicangelo, Fr. Peter Lentine of St. Philomena, Vittorio Re, Salvatore Palazzolo, Anthony Palazzolo, Concetta Alesiak, Vita Corrado, Domenico Mancini, Marlene Baker, William Battaglia, Post 570, Albert and Mary Fontana, Sam Scalisi, Emmanuel Gravame, Jenny Catalfio, Joann Frederick, Greg Cipriano, Armando Delicato, Maria Lamia, Fr. Carl Bonk of SS. Peter and Paul, David Miros, Northwest Jesuit archives, Archdiocese of Detroit, Fr. Mike Green of St. Scholastica, Joe Provenzano, Fr. Edward Vilkauskas of St. Mary's, the Burton Historical staff, Antonia Valentine, Grace Perrone, Joe Toia, Carol Palazzolo, Rosalie House, Catherine Bagnasco, Annette Cipriano, Tony Badalamenti, Lena Locricchio, Angie Vitale, Charlie Bono, Kathy Stercum, Sarah Stork, Elisabeth Megna, Peter Ferro, Sam Genovese, Dr. Sal Ventimiglia, Johnnie Woolsey, Sebastiano Previti, Linda Davis, and anyone else I may have forgotten.

# INTRODUCTION

The cornerstone of SS. Peter and Paul's Jesuit Church was laid on June 29, 1844, under the guidance of Bishop Peter Paul Lefebvre, who served as the second bishop of the city of Detroit from 1841 until his death in March 1869. The church was originally the cathedral of the Archdiocese of Detroit.

SS. Peter and Paul is now the oldest church building in the city still standing in its original form. Bishop Lefebvre's successor, Bishop Casper Borgess, gave the title for the building to the Society of Jesus (the Jesuit order) in 1877, as part of an agreement under which the Jesuits would undertake to build the first catholic college, which became the University of Detroit.

In 1900, the area around SS. Peter and Paul, on Jefferson Avenue, Larned Street, Congress Street, and Fort Street, between Brush Street and Hastings Street, started seeing an influx of Italians. Southern Italians and Sicilians began settling into this elite and quiet area, home to French and English lawyers, writers, engineers, and other professional households. The Sicilian population, steadily increasing within these parish boundaries, was originally administered by Fr. Eugene Kieffer, who had taken special notice of these immigrants when they flocked to his church, devoting himself to their spiritual needs. Father Kieffer started to learn Italian, but it was beginning to get harder and harder for him to tend to the needs of all of his parishioners.

Father Kieffer expressed the need for assistance to Bishop John Foley and, in turn, Bishop Foley informed the Archbishop Falconi, the delegate in Washington, D.C., who then wrote to Pope Pius X on August 2, 1905, explaining the situation: out of the 17 priests at the Jesuit church and college, not one could speak Italian. If they had a priest who spoke the language of these newcomers and understood their cultural needs, a church could be built for them, eliminating further problems. Alternatively, Bishop Foley would have to consider dividing the parish. Pope Pius X agreed to provide an administrator, stating that the spiritual welfare of the Italian Americans should be protected. Archbishop Falconi sent copies of the papal message to all bishops and heads of orders, looking for a priest. The Jesuit's father provincial finally realized that the situation demanded his attention and that the natives of southern Italy had no suitable place of worship; San Francesco Church was located further north in the city and served a mainly northern Italian institution. The provincial promised to send someone to take care of the Southern Italians. Until the church could be built, the parishioners were divided, and the Sicilians worshipped in a small chapel located on the property of SS. Peter and Paul.

At the close of 1905, a priest was sent: Fr. Raffaele D'Orsi. Father D'Orsi was called out of a mission in Denver to formulate plans for a new parish under the guidance of Bishop Foley.

Father D'Orsi was born in Naples, Italy, in 1858. He left Naples when he was 15, later joining the Jesuit order in 1873. Upon arrival in the United States, D'Orsi worked in missions in the Southwest.

Detroit was Father D'Orsi's first big city. He quickly found that working among the Italians was not so easy; they had come from a land where the government maintained and funded churches indirectly through taxation. The idea of funding a church themselves with their own money, with no contract or promises, was new and difficult, especially since they had no one they truly trusted in the new land. Father D'Orsi did not have the necessary patience and stayed less than a year.

Several months after Father D'Orsi left, there seemed to be little hope. Efforts to form a parish seemed unlikely to succeed as the Sicilians began to argue among themselves, blaming each other for their difficulties. That was until Fr. Giovanni Boschi arrived. In mid-1907, Francesca Carta, Jim Vadalabene, and others longing for a church in the new homeland quickly acquainted themselves with Father Boschi, explaining their difficulty in raising money from the people to build a church. It was not that they were greedy, but they did not understand the "American way" of investing in things without a contract or a guarantee.

Father Boschi started calling, door to door, with Jim Vadalabene and found that there were nearly 3,000 Sicilians within the parish boundaries. Over the next few months, he made many friends. People were starting to trust him, and a meeting was held on December 7, 1907, in the hall of SS. Peter and Paul Church, at which time a committee of 30 men was formed.

Joseph Giulanda was elected president; Francesco Paolo D'Anna was elected vice president; Joseph Mazzola was elected secretary; and the other members of the committee included Joseph Moceri, Carlo Ciamataro, Francesco Carta, Giuseppe Tranchida, Salvatore Zerilli, James LoCocco, Antonio Tedesco, Peter Leto, James and Vincent Vadalabene, Benedetto Segesta, Francesco Mancuso, Vito Aleccia, Filippo Guastella, Domenic Grillo, Pietro Mirabile, Francesco Dicausi, Paolo Ferrara, Calagero Mannino, Salvatore Taormina, Charley Gardella, Pietra Bellanca, Antonio Catalano, Cristoforo Mangiapane, Luciano Gambino, Luigi Reguli, and Giuseppe Stabile. At the same time, the fraternal order of San Giuseppe was formed to act as the collectors of the funds needed to build a church.

Over the next few months these men went out into the streets, usually in teams, soliciting money. The average wage at the time was 11¢ an hour, and their average monthly collection was just under $370. When they raised nearly $2,000, they purchased a lot for $4,000 from Mary Mix at the corner of Hastings and Fort Streets, giving her a deposit of $1,137.

When Bishop Foley saw that the people were coming together, he installed Father Boschi fully as administrator and priest over the Sicilian people, celebrating mass out of the solidarity chapel of SS. Peter and Paul. Bishop Foley officially established the parish of Holy Family on April 7, 1908, and it was designated a Sicilian church. The first baptism performed in the parish was for Vincenzo Licavoli, son of Giuseppe Licavoli and Rosalia Pagano, and the first marriage in the parish was of Salvatore Giordano and Rosa Evola, both of families from Terrasini, Sicily.

In August 1909, Father Boschi wrote to Bishop Foley asking that they be allowed to start work on the church by September so that they would be able to celebrate the laying of the cornerstone on the feast day of our Lady of the Rosary, which would fall on October 3. Father Boschi estimated that it would cost $15,000; he would collect $5,000 and borrow $10,000. Father Boschi told Bishop Foley that the Italians had promised to continue monthly collections until the debt had been paid; a contingency plan would ensure repayment within three years. Father Boschi pleaded that the work must begin or the people would lose confidence; they had paid for the land and nothing was happening.

The bishop still did not give his approval. Father Boschi wrote again on September 8, 1909, with a plan to borrow $12,000 from Wayne Bank by mortgaging the lot, and if need be the new building. He planned to use $2,000 to purchase a second lot for security. The bishop did not interfere, and by mid-October parishioners had begun to pitch in with labor to dig the foundation. Vito Aleccia donated funds and worked for two weeks; and Giuseppe Agnello,

Filippo Guastella, and Giuseppe Stablie were just a few of the many men to contribute unpaid labor to build a church of their own.

By December 5, 1909, the foundation had been completed and the cornerstone laid, with a ceremony to celebrate the moment. The formalities began with the Grand Knights of St. John escorting Bishop Foley from his residence on Washington Boulevard to SS. Peter and Paul at St. Antoine Street and Jefferson Avenue where the services were held; then the parade began and the parishioners and societies marched to the new church grounds. Francesco Finnegan served as grand marshal; and participants included the St. Joseph's Boys Band, the Knights of St. John's, the Italian band, the Lombardi Society, the Union and Brotherhood, the San Francesco Society, the Savoia Society, the Trinchia Society, the Sacred Heart Society, and the St. Joseph Society.

By May 23, 1910, money was running short and Father Boschi was driven to mortgage the church to borrow $5,060.75 in order to complete the building. On November 13, 1910, the church building at 129 Hastings Street was finally completed. The Chiesa della Sacra Famiglia opened with a glorious mass led by Father Boschi and music performed by an orchestra directed by Maestro Valle with a grand *festa* following. The following Sunday, the first official sacrament took place: the baptism of Elena Zerilli, daughter of Anthony Zerilli and Philappa Lafata.

Over the next few years the Sicilians clashed with Bishop Foley, who felt they should conform to the local American religious practices. Bishop Foley denied burial to a man because he did not attend church regularly; he would not allow parishioners to use the Italian flag in the church; and he did not want parishioners to participate in processions carrying statues, a tradition dear to the hearts of immigrants who still valued the traditions of their home country and religion. In 1917, Fr. Petronio Zagni was brought in to assist Father Parodi, whose health was failing. Father Parodi soon retired, but parishioners still wanted to confess to him. Soon thereafter, Father Boschi's health failed as well, and he was sent to Holy Family Church in San Jose, California, where he died three years later.

Father Zagni was now solely administrating the spiritual needs of 15,000 Southern Italians in the parish boundaries. Bishop Foley's death on January 5, 1918, exacerbated Father Zagni's problems and the Jesuits did not have a solution. In June 1919, Father Zagni was transferred to Cleveland, and an Augustinian father who knew very little Italian took his place. The Sicilians demanded his removal and blocked entrance to the church, demanding Father Zagni's return. Father Zagni was sent back. In September, after the feast of Madonna delle Grazie, Father Zagni and the Augustinian stole away in the night, locking the church doors, never to return again. The doors were locked for two weeks, until a delegation from the Italian societies went to newly installed Bishop Michael Gallagher, who had already dismissed them as an obtrusive presence. Bishop Michael Gallagher wanted them to abandon their culture and traditions too. The Sicilians refused and were assigned temporary priests throughout the next year.

In September 1920, the archdiocese finally gave the Holy Family congregation a priest. Fr. John Vismara was a native Detroiter of Italian descent and would be pastor for the next seven years. The Sicilian population was nearing 20,000 and growing, even as many Sicilians moved north toward Highland Park where the second Sicilian church, Santa Maria, was built in 1919. The parish was overwhelming for Father Vismara; another church was needed. Father Vismara pleaded to have the parish boundaries adjusted so that some of his flock could also use St. Joachim— the French in the area were moving out as the Sicilians moved in and the priest at St. Joachim was only servicing a handful of parishioners. The diocese sent Fr. Anthony DeSantis to assist Father Vismara, along with a handful of other priests over the next several years.

The archdiocese no longer wanted to service Holy Family Church and asked the Benedictine order to help. On January 1, 1929, the Benedictines took responsibility for Holy Family, and they serviced the parish for the next 76 years, providing some of the finest priests, all of whom were of Italian descent. The last Benedictine pastor was Fr. John Stopponi, who died in November 2005. He had come out of retirement to service the parish after the death of Fr. Noel Patacconi in 1996.

Today parishioners may feel that history repeats itself. The Benedictines no longer service Holy Family, and the parish was left without a priest. The diocese, in administration of the parish again after an interim of many decades, still wants the parishioners to adapt their culture and traditions to the American norm. Society leaders have asked for a priest to serve Holy Family, and their requests have been rejected. As of 2008, the parish shares an administrator—Fr. Edward Vilkauskas—with the neighboring St. Mary's. Parishioners depend on Fr. Lawrence Fares, a retired diocesan priest, to give Sunday masses. The surrounding neighborhoods are long gone, but times have not changed so much. La Chiesa della Sacra Famiglia still stands, now nestled between parking structures and downtown office buildings, still rich in culture and tradition. Viva Maria. Viva San Giuseppe. Viva La Sacra Famiglia.

# One

# THE CHURCH

Since the parish was first organized, in 1908, it has been tradition for Italian and Sicilian families to return to Holy Family Church for their sacraments, even if they do not attend the church regularly. The wedding of Ciro Poma and Giovanna Pace is pictured; Fr. Noel Patacconi officiated. (Giovanna Poma.)

SS. Peter and Paul's Jesuit Church, located on Jefferson Avenue, is the oldest church building in Detroit, built in 1844. Once the cathedral of the Archdiocese of Detroit and a second home to a congregation of predominantly French and Irish parishioners, SS. Peter and Paul drew Sicilians arriving in Detroit until the Jesuits built them a church of their own. Today Fr. Carl Bonk, S.J., is the pastor of SS. Peter and Paul and is responsible for many outreach programs. (Burton Historical Collection.)

The 400th anniversary of the Jesuit order was celebrated in October 1940 in the grand sanctuary of SS. Peter and Paul. (Burton Historical Collection.)

Over the years, as priests changed, so did the interior of the church. At the wedding of James Patti and Concetta Cusmano in 1946, the interior of the church is decorated with one small mural of a dove above the altar and chandeliers. The pulpit area and the altar rail are painted to resemble marble. Over the years the church would be further adorned with decorative art and glorious paintings. (Concetta Alesiak.)

Fr. Benedict Ferretti was the first priest to change the trim art and to put a full mural over the altar, as seen in this photograph taken in 1955 at the wedding of Luke Vitale and Angeline Lunardo. (Angie Vitale.)

When Fr. Bonfil Alexander Bottazzo became pastor of Holy Family in the 1960s, changes were made in the interior murals. Pictured here are angels over the altar at the 1978 wedding of Anthony Viviani and Karleen Bleggi. The old wooden rail was replaced with marble, donated in the memory of Domenico and Francesca Salafia. (Tony and Karleen Viviani.)

In the 1980s, under Fr. Noel Patacconi, the artistic contributions of Father Bonfil and Fr. Maurus Michelini were painted over and even more murals were painted covering almost every inch of the church. The artist was Angelo Lanzini, and eight of the picture panels were donated by Humprey and Celine Tocco, Dominic and Jenny Riggio, Tom Maceri and Sons, the Olivastri family, Lee BeGole, Carl and Eleanora Bommarito, M. A. W., and J. H. S. and J. A. K. (Author's collection.)

Vito and Rose Giacalone donated the statues of St. Rosalia and St. Vito at the rear of the church, and in 1961, the pews were given by the family of Giacomo and Nina Giacalone in their memory. (Author's collection.)

The cars photographed here are decorated for the wedding of William Fanfalone and Doris Balsamo in 1949. The cars are parked in front of Holy Family Church, which was located at the corner of East Fort and Hastings Streets. East Fort Street no longer exists, and the 129 Hastings Street address is now 641 Chrysler Highway. (Doris Fanfalone.)

In 1963, when the construction of the Walter P. Chrysler Freeway was underway, Sacra Famiglia was spared the wrecking ball due to the efforts of the men pictured below, along with others. These men have earned the respect of generations to come, and their descendants continue to enjoy their sacraments, Italian feast days, and Latin traditions in the church that their ancestors built and worshipped in. (Burton Historical Collection.)

These strong and influential men took over where their ancestors left off, doing anything necessary to keep their church, history, and traditions intact while every street and building directly around the church was demolished for downtown development and freeways. Pictured from left to right are Anthony Corrado, Anthony Bagnasco, Joseph Randazzo, Anthony D'Anna, Fr. Noel Patacconi, Vince Palazzola, Sam Biondo, Carl Bommarito, Jack Tocco, and Sam Lafata. (Carl and Eleanora Bommarito.)

16

After the 1967 riots the city was almost ruined. A group of businessmen came together to try to find a way to save the city. Henry Ford II proposed a plan to Mayor Roman Gribbs. At a cost of $500 million, they would develop the riverfront and build Michigan's tallest building, the largest privately financed project in the world. By 1976, the 73-story building known as the Renaissance Center was complete and became a towering backdrop for the church. (Holy Family.)

Sometime in the late 1970s, when the expressway was finished and the dust had stopped flying from construction of the 22-story Blue Cross building at 600 East Lafayette Street, the church was painted for the first time. No one considered the issue of maintenance costs: about $40,000 each time the church is fully repainted. (Burton Historical Collection.)

The original steps of the church could hold nearly 50 people. This group photograph was taken at the wedding of Michael Megna and Elizabeth Imbrunone in 1947. (Elizabeth Megna.)

Today the front entrance looks much different due to renovations undertaken by a dedicated group. Curt Colo, pictured on the left, contributed concrete steps; Joe Bommarito refinished the brass rails; Joe DeMaria put in new lighting; Belle Isle replaced the awning; Robert Stalling and his crew refinished the doors and painted the entrance; and Brian Valenti created the new stone surface for the steps. (Author's collection.)

The kneelers, covers, priest vestments, and altar cloths pictured here are still in use today; many of these items were hand sewn and beaded by Marianna Finazzo. Photographed kneeling in 1949 are, from left to right, Anthony Crimuda, Harry Serra, James and Sarah Stork, Rose Laduca, and Josephine Serra. (Sarah Stork.)

Hastings Street, across from the church, is photographed in the 1940s during the feast day procession of Madonna delle Grazie. There were many stores with upper flats and a full neighborhood of homes around this block, where the freeway now lies. (Rosary Amore.)

This is the wedding of Luke Vitale and Angie Lunardo. Members of the wedding party had fun after the ceremony decorating their cars and driving around the neighborhood honking their horns. Today this scene has changed, limousines and sometimes even buses are the transportation of choice. (Angie Vitale.)

This photograph was taken in 1990, the year that Holy Family Church was designated a Michigan state historic site. Michigan's secretary of state Richard Austin (at left) is pictured with Stephen Maniaci of Post 570. Fr. Noel Patacconi and Post 570 were instrumental in garnering the designation. They celebrated this day with high mass and a luncheon; the honor of unveiling the plaque was given to Rosina Bommarito, the oldest living parishioner at the time. (Holy Family.)

*Two*

# THE PRIESTS

Bishop John Foley, born on November 5, 1833, in Baltimore, Maryland, became a priest in 1856 and was appointed fourth bishop to the Archdiocese of Detroit on November 4, 1888. At first, after Pope Pius X sent a papal message saying that the Italian American culture should be protected, Bishop Foley was instrumental in helping to form the Holy Family parish. Later on, however, he often clashed with the Sicilians, as they sometimes did not conform to local religious practices. Bishop Foley died on January 5, 1918. (Archdiocese of Detroit.)

Founding priest Fr. Giovanni Boschi, S.J., pictured in the second row at far right, was born in 1862 in Bertinoro, Italy. He entered the Jesuit Society in 1882 and came to Detroit in 1907 to establish a parish for the Sicilians attending SS. Peter and Paul's Jesuit Church. Father Boschi made friends quickly. Within two years, the Sicilians had a church of their own. Due to poor health, Father Boschi was sent to California, where he died in 1921. (Midwest Jesuit Archives.)

Fr. Aloysius Luigi Parodi, S.J., was born in Genoa, Italy, in 1846; entered the Jesuit Society in 1878; and was educated in Europe. Father Parodi (first row, fourth from left) labored in the northwest Native American missions for 20 years, spent 9 years with the Inuit in Alaska, and spent 19 years among the Sicilians in Detroit. Father Parodi wrote wonderful poems and stories for people for special occasions and holidays and was a caring priest to whom the parishioners flocked even after his retirement. Father Parodi died on April 15, 1928. (Midwest Jesuit Archives.)

Fr. John Vismara, D.D., was born on June 5, 1886, in Detroit, to Angelo and Rachel Mary, one of the first northern Italian families to settle in Detroit, in 1881. The Vismaras had three sons, all of whom graduated from the University of Detroit, and three daughters. Father Vismara, an avid writer, completed much of his seminary study in Rome. He was ordained in 1909 and spent his first 10 years in Kalamazoo. In 1920, after the Jesuit fathers had given up Holy Family, the diocese felt that Father Vismara was the only priest equipped to administer the parish, due to his Italian roots. He remained at Holy Family for seven years and was administrator at St. Catherine of Siena until he died on June 3, 1952, while visiting Rome and his good friend Monsieur Dante, an assistant to the pope. (Burton Historical Collection.)

Fr. Anthony DeSantis, D.D., an archdiocesan priest, took over for a short period when Father Vismara moved to another parish. Father DeSantis first came in 1918 as assistant priest and became pastor in 1925; he was pastor until 1927, when the diocese was no longer able to allow for a permanent full-time priest for the parish. There was a two-year period during which the parish was without a pastor, until 1929, when the Benedictine order decided to serve Holy Family Church. (Archdiocese of Detroit.)

Fr. Alberic Maggiore, O.S.B., the first Benedictine priest to serve Holy Family, was pastor from 1929 until 1931. The Benedictines served Holy Family for 76 years, with some of the finest Italian priests the parishioners had the opportunity to worship under. Today, for the first time in history, Holy Family is served by a non-Italian priest. (St. Scholastica.)

At the age of 12, Fr. Benedict Ferretti, O.S.B., was an altar boy in his hometown of Fabriano (Paterno), Italy. Although Benedict's widowed mother wanted her son to go to technical school, the pastor of their church asked her to allow him to attend retreats with the monks at Montetano. She agreed, and by the age of 16, Ferretti was prepared to become a monk. He studied in Rome and was ordained in 1931. In 1932, Father Ferretti was sent to Holy Family Church and remained for 34 years. Father Ferretti was appointed superior of the Holy Face Monastery in New Jersey, where he died in 1983. He is buried at St. Benedict Monastery in Oxford, Michigan. (Mary Lou Kulakowski.)

Fr. Joseph Muzzin, O.S.B., was born in Italy in 1920. He joined the Benedictine order at 11 and was ordained in 1944. Father Muzzin came to Holy Family Church in 1947 and served as an assistant priest until 1952. He then served at St. Scholastica in Monroe. Known as "Father Joe," Father Muzzin was a well-mannered priest who enjoyed good wine and food. He was never too busy to take a call, and parishioners treated him like family. Father Muzzin returned to Holy Family in 1981 and remained until his death in 1992. He is buried at the monastery in Oxford. (Holy Family.)

Fr. Bonfil Alexander Bottazzo, O.S.B., was first assistant priest at Holy Family in 1949. When Father Ferretti went to Italy on sabbatical in 1959, Father Bottazzo became pastor. He was a caring man and was able to accomplish much with the help of the Italian societies; in the 1960s, he was able to build a new rectory. In the 1980s, Father Bottazzo left Holy Family and the Benedictine order and was incarnated to the Lansing diocese. (Archdiocese of Detroit.)

Fr. Giovanni Lucenti (second from left), O.S.B., was assistant pastor at Holy Family from 1951 to 1957. A handsome and bright man with a saintly glow, Father Lucenti now lives in the San Silvestro Monestary in Italy. (St. Scholastica.)

Fr. Anselm Vissani, O.S.B., born in Poggio South Vicino, Italy, in 1894, joined the Sylvestrian Benedictine order in 1910. He served in the Italian army during World War I and was ordained at a mission in Ceylon in 1922. In 1937, Father Vissani came to Holy Family and served until 1948, when he was elected procurator general of the order in Rome. In 1958, Father Vissani was stationed at the Holy Face Monastery in New Jersey, where he died in 1962. Father Vissani's remains were returned to Holy Family for a requiem mass, laid to rest at Holy Sepulchre Catholic Cemetery, and later moved to the monastery in Oxford. (St. Scholastica.)

Fr. Maurus Michelini, O.S.B., came to Holy Family in 1962 and served as assistant pastor until 1966. Father Michelini particularly enjoyed Italian feast days. He helped with organization and planning for the new courtyard and many of the first murals in the church. Father Michelini spent the last years of his life at San Vincenzo Monastery, in Italy, and died on August 17, 2004. (Holy Family.)

Noel Patacconi, O.S.B., was born in Ancona, Italy, on December 24, 1908, and came to the United States in 1933. Ordained in 1932, Father Patacconi served as assistant pastor at Our Lady of Help, where many Sicilians attended school, from 1933 until 1953, and as pastor from 1953 through 1963, after which he moved to the Benedictine Monastery in Oxford, Michigan. Father Patacconi became pastor of Holy Family Church in 1972 and remained until his death in 1996. In 1989, Father Patacconi was instrumental in having the church designated a state historical site. He wrote articles for the *Italian Tribune* and *American Home*. He was also quite a carpenter. Father Patacconi is buried at the monastery in Oxford. (Helen Brennan.)

Fr. John Stopponi, born on January 16, 1914, in Abacina, Italy, was called to the priesthood at 11 and went to a monastery founded by Sylvester Gazzolini in the 13th century. Father Stopponi was from a family of two monks, two nuns, and a Franciscan priest. He was ordained in 1938 and came to the United States in 1948. He spent several years as the pastor of St. Angela Merici Parish in Canada. In 1963, Father Stopponi became pastor of Our Lady of Help, and he resigned in 1967 just before the parish closed on its 100th anniversary. Father Stopponi retired in 1981, but he returned to Holy Family after the death of Father Patacconi and stayed until his death on November 27, 2005. (Holy Family.)

After the death of Fr. John Stopponi, an emergency meeting was held and Fr. Ken Kaucheck—vicar of the Renaissance Vicariate and pastor of Our Lady Star of the Sea—was appointed temporary administrator; Lee Begole was appointed parish council president. Lori McGlinnen, associate director of parish life for the Archdiocese of Detroit, assisted at the meeting. A mural in the church hall depicting an ancient Roman scene served as an appropriate backdrop. (Author's collection.)

Fr. Lawrence Fares, born in North Lebanon in 1924, was ordained in Rome in 1950. Pope Paul VI declared him apostolic missionary to various Asian and Middle Eastern locales, and he built and served Holy Family Church in Kuwait. Father Fares, who speaks numerous languages, has been in the United States since 1969. He is now retired from the Archdiocese of Detroit but services the masses at Holy Family each Sunday even though he is not the pastor. (Fr. Lawrence Fares.)

Fr. Edward Vikauskas, ordained in 1973, has master's degrees in theology and liturgical studies, much of his schooling spent in London. A Spiritan, or Holy Ghost Father, Father Vikauskas spent 12 years in North Carolina and is now pastor of Old St. Mary's Church in Detroit's Greektown. He was appointed administrator of Holy Family in an emergency decision by Cardinal Maida in July 2006. (Father Vikauskas.)

On St. Joseph's Day in 2006, Bishop John Quinn was the bearer of disappointing news. The Holy Family Parish would not be given Fr. Eduard Perrone as administrator. Members of the parish had longed for the leadership of the Italian priest, who is the pastor at Assumption Grotto; it was felt that Father Perrone would understand their culture and traditions because of his ancestral ties to the church. Cardinal Maida rejected the parish request and named Father Vilkauskas of Old St. Mary's the administrator on the basis of locality. Father Perrone (second from left) and Bishop Quinn (center) were photographed at the grotto. (Assumption Grotto.)

In 1987, Pope John Paul II came to Michigan, stopping in Hamtramck, a predominantly Polish community. Fr. John Stopponi was able to meet the pope; it was a day that was dear to Father Stopponi's heart. Pope John Paul II was one of the longest-reigning popes in history, serving from October 16, 1978, to April 2, 2005, when he died at age 84. (Holy Family.)

# *Three*

# FOUNDING FAMILIES

Early parishioners
Alessandro Ciaramitaro and
his wife, Pauline LaRosa,
married on February 2,
1908, at the Cathedral
Mazara del Vallo in the
province of Trapani. This
picture was taken shortly
after their arrival in
Detroit in November 1908.
Pauline was pregnant and
very ill from the 16-day
trip over rough water; to
Pauline it felt like months.
(Emmanuel Gravame.)

Francesco Carta and his family first settled in Detroit in 1902. One of the original founders of the parish of Holy Family Church, as well as Santa Maria (formed south of Highland Park), Carta opened a grocery store at 193 Monroe Street. Carta is pictured here with his wife, Rosalia Mirabella, and their children, from left to right, Joseph, Mary, Frances, Michael, Pauline, and Leo. (Frank and Josephine Carta.)

The Moceri family members are pictured from left to right in their first family photograph taken in Detroit, in 1900: (first row) Vicenza (Moceri) Ciaramitaro, Justina (Moceri) Palazzolo, Concetta (Locricchio) Moceri holding "Momo" Moceri with son Domenico Moceri on the floor, Francesca (Moceri) Aijello, Antonia (Orlando) Moceri holding Cola Moceri with son Domenico Moceri sitting, and Justina Moceri standing with baby Grazia Moceri in the high chair; (second row) Grazia (Moceri) Licavoli, James Moceri, Francesco Palazzola, Joseph Moceri, Chiro Aijello, and Domenico Moceri. (Rosary Amore.)

One of the founding families, Giovanni Parisi and his wife, Rosina Corsot, came to the United States through St. Louis in 1898. They joined the parish when their third daughter, Providentia, was baptized in 1910, and they baptized a baby girl every two years, becoming the proud parents of "the Parisi eight." This photograph was taken on the day of their daughter Grace's marriage to Jim Capizzo. Pictured from left to right are (first row) Phyllis Briguglio, Sarah, Laurain Giorlando, and Augustine Parisi; (second row) Pearl, Frances Briguglio, baby Fanny, Jim, Grace, Josephine Giorlando, and Rose; and (third row) Mike Briguglio, Rose, Lena, Giovanni, and Joe Giorlando. (Sara Scrivano.)

Early parishioner names are inscribed on the founders' plaque, now in great need of repair. Peter Pellerito came to the United States in the early 1900s and married Angela Cilluffo in 1903. They had four children, the fourth baptized in the church soon after construction was completed in 1910. Three of their four children were married at Holy Family. (DiMaggio family.)

Antonio Tedesco, born in Sicily in 1862, came to Detroit in 1890 with his wife, Domenica Catalona, and lived down the street from SS. Peter and Paul at 118 St. Antoine Street. By 1894, Tedesco had started his own produce business. Tedesco was in the first 30 men active in forming the Holy Family Parish. He and his wife's families both donated stained-glass windows to the parish in 1910. The Tedescos were the parents of nine children, all born in Detroit. By 1912, their daughter Angela had been married in the newly constructed church to Salvatore Moceri. Antonio and Domenica are pictured here with their oldest child, Joachim, who was born in 1903. (Sandra [Tedesco] Smith.)

Joseph Mazzola came to the United States from Terrasini, Sicily. In December 1907, he became the first secretary for the committee of men comprising the fraternal order of St. Joseph, who built the parish of Holy Family Church. Mazzola helped collect the funds needed to build the church. He married Rose Cusmano, and they had four sons and three daughters. (Joseph Mazzola.)

Theresa (Gravame) Lafata was baptized at Holy Family in 1912, the daughter of Emanuel Gravame and Maria Resa, one of the first families in the parish. This is Theresa in 1925 on her first visit back to her father's homeland—Taranto, Italy. Theresa is proudly adorned with her uncle's Italian navy hat and flag. (Emmanuel Gravame.)

*Elizabeth Falsone*

This beautiful woman, Elizabeth Falsone, was not given the chance to live a long and full life, but the life she did live was centered on the church and raising her children. She was one of the early parishioners and one of the first members of Madonna di Trapani and the Holy Face Society. (Liz Falsone.)

35

Francesco Culotta came to Detroit in the early 1900s and first worshipped, as did most Sicilians, at SS. Peter and Paul. Culotta married Lucia Ristiva. One of the first parishioners at Holy Family, in 1910, Culotta paid for the first communion rail in the church; it was made out of wood and painted to resemble marble. (William Battaglia.)

Maria Culotta is still living, at the age of 101. The daughter of Francesco Culotta and Lucia Ristiva, Maria was photographed sitting on her mother's lap; she holds a purse she still has today. Maria was born on March 21, 1907, and was baptized in May of the same year, just after the arrival of Father Boschi, who served the Sicilians at SS. Peter and Paul. (William Battaglia.)

Augustina, the daughter of Augustino Culotta and his wife, Maria Rocco, was one of the first babies baptized in the parish of Holy Family—on November 1, 1908. In 1910, Augustino bought one of the first stained-glass windows for the church. (William Battaglia.)

This stained-glass window depicting the Immaculata was given to Holy Family by Augustino Culotta in 1910 at a cost of $37 per window. Today to repair a small hole in this same window costs $400. (Author's collection.)

Pictured are Holy Family founders Peter Leto and Pietrina Palazzolo. Leto came to the United States in 1901 at the age of 13. He and his wife were married for more than 60 years. Leto was one of the builders working on construction of the church and first rectory. He owned and operated the Leto Building Company for more than 50 years. Leto belonged to the Knights of Columbus, Sacred Heart, and St. Joseph's Society and donated one of the first stained-glass windows installed in the church. (Peter, Paul, and Grace [Leto] Tocco.)

Born in 1885, Gaetano Guastella of Alcamo, Sicily, and his brother Filippo were among the first parishioners of Holy Family. Filippo was one of the first men on the committee to form the parish and donated both money and hard labor to the building of the church. Gaetano arrived in Detroit and helped put the finishing touches on the church and rectory. Gaetano and his wife, Josephine Salerno, married in 1913 and renewed their vows—after 50 years of marriage—in 1963 at Holy Family. (Joann Frederick.)

# *Four*

# THEIR LIVES

Domenico Moceri came to the United States in 1894 with his wife, Antonia Orlando, and their children Domenico and Justina. By 1898 they had two more children, Cola and Grace. Domenico started his produce business on this wagon. Antonia died in 1908, and Domenico returned to Italy, where he married Rosaria Cali. Domenico's brother Joseph kept the business going until his return. Domenico was blessed with several more sons, and by 1918 his Moceri Brothers Fruits venture operated a one-ton truck. (Rosary Amore.)

Francesco Culotta (third from left) is pictured with his son Charlie (sixth from left), and his son Joe (ninth from left) in 1931 at his warehouse in the Eastern Market. Culotta started with a vegetable cart and worked his way up to a warehouse as partner in Culotta and Jull Produce. (William Battaglia.)

After his father Antonio's death in 1948, parishioner Joachim Tedesco continued in the business that his father had started after he arrived in Detroit in 1894. Joachim, born in 1903, married Bella McMaster. They were happily married for more than 70 years. Joachim is pictured here with his only child, Antonio, in his wholesale fruit market at 262 East Fort Street. Today Tedesco's produce operation is in its fifth generation. (Sandra [Tedesco] Smith.)

Joseph Moceri, born in 1869, was a founding member of the parish. Joseph peddled fruit from a cart for his brother Domenico after his arrival in Detroit from Terrasini in 1900. Joseph is photographed here (left) many years later in his own market. He died at the age of 64, leaving his family and the church he worked so hard to build. (Joe D'Anna.)

One of the early parishioners of the church, Vincenzo DiMaggio is sitting (center) with friends and family on a Sunday afternoon. Sundays were typically the only day of the week on which a Sicilian male could take time to relax. Vincenzo married Maria Maisano, and they had two sons and two daughters. For a short period he lived and worked in the coal mines in Adrian, commuting back and forth to the city. (DiMaggio family.)

Our Lady of Help Parish was built in 1867 and run by the same Benedictine fathers who served Holy Family; many Sicilian children later went to school at Our Lady of Help. Congregants often worshipped in both the parish of Our Lady of Help and Holy Family. Our Lady of Help closed in 1967 and was demolished the following year. (St. Scholastica.)

The societies supporting Holy Family had wanted to build a school for their children, but the bishop would not allow it. In the early years, the children of the parish attended SS. Peter and Paul and then, as the population grew, St. Mary's. Some children attended St. Joseph's and Our Lady of Help, and as the Sicilian community expanded to the east, children began to attend St. Margaret Mary and Our Lady of Sorrows. Our Lady of Sorrows's sixth-grade class of 1937 is pictured. (DiMaggio family.)

Today two miracles attributed to Fr. Noel Patacconi are still remembered. During World War II, Father Patacconi led the parishioners in solemn prayer, asking that those serving might all come home alive; if their prayers were answered, the parishioners promised to build a spectacular shrine in honor of Mary, Jesus, the saints they prayed to, and all those saved. Their prayers were answered, and the shrine was built. The brickwork and pillars for the shrine were laid by Emanuel Gravame, one of Holy Family's first parishioners. The second miracle occurred during Father Patacconi's journey overseas. An enemy submarine had fired a torpedo, and Father Patacconi instructed the panicking travelers in prayer. The torpedo turned back to hit the enemy submarine that had fired. (Holy Family.)

This is the 1930 eighth grade class at Old St. Mary's, where Holy Family parishioner Frances Moceri went to school. In her class was a boy who would become mayor of the city of Detroit, Coleman A. Young. He would often go to the Moceri's on Sundays to grab a bite to eat. Moceri is in the first row, right, and Young is in the second row, third from right. (Joe D'Anna.)

In a long-standing tradition, after the ceremony wedding parties would group up in cars to go to another location to take photographs. One of the hottest spots was Belle Isle—originally called Isle aux Cochons, or "hog island." Belle Isle's James Scott Memorial Fountain is still a favorite spot for photographs. In 1910, upon the death of gambler James Scott, $500,000 was bequeathed to have a statue and a fountain built and dedicated to his memory. Because of his reputation, it took the city 15 years to decide if they wanted to build it. Pictured from left to right are Sam Todaro, Maureen ?, Vito Moceri, Josephine DeMaria, groom Luke Vitale, bride Angeline Lunardo, Joe Vitale, Grace Vitale, Sam Vitale, and Beatrice ?. (Angie Vitale.)

Josephine (Maniaci) Biundo was baptized at Holy Family in 1921. A weak baby, not expected to live and never making a sound, on the Sunday she was born, Josephine's parents, Antonio Maniaci and Fara Cilluffo, ran to the church with her during mass. Fr. John Vismara saw that the family was in despair and offered to baptize the baby. As he sprinkled water across the baby's head she began to cry. To this day, Josie is a devout Catholic. Pictured here during the 1940s, Josie enjoys the view at Belle Isle. (Josephine Biundo.)

Frank Bagnasco was born in Terrasini, Sicily, in 1891. At nine years old he was cutting hair as a barber, and by the age of 14 he had became an undertaker to the Sicilians. The son of Salvatore Bagnnsco and Providentia Orlando, Frank married Brigitta Fodale in 1915 at Holy Family Church. Frank belonged to several Italian societies and was widely known for his charitable enterprises. (Bill Bagnasco.)

**Unico Undertaker Italiano In Citta'**

Funerali a meta' del costo. Bellissime casse mortuarie in nero o in altri colori, guarnite in argento per $25,00. Altre casse a prezzi ridotti.

Chiamateci a qualunque momento giorno o notte. Perche' pagate di piu' quando noi possiamo farvi il miglior servizio e darvi i migliori oggetti a meta' prezzo di quello che altri undertaker domanderebbero'

# Frank Bagnasco Co.

261 - 266 Rivard St.         Telefono Cadillac 2356 J

La Tribuna costa solo un dollaro all'anno

This advertisement from 1914 for Frank Bagnasco's funeral home reads, "The only Italian undertaker in the city. Funerals at half the cost. Beautiful caskets in black and other colors. Trimmed in silver for $25.00. Other caskets at lower prices. Call us at any time day or night. Why pay more when we can provide a better service and give you better quality at half the price that other undertakers would give you?" It cost only $1 a year to advertise in the *Italian Tribune*. As their fathers before them, today Frank's grandchildren carry on his business and support many ventures at Holy Family Church. (Bill Bagnasco.)

Joseph Moceri was among the first 30 men who formed the parish of Holy Family. Moceri's wife, Concetta (Locricchio) Moceri, is pictured here. Concetta was godmother to over a dozen children and a caretaker to Sicilians who came to Detroit with no place else to go. Concetta and Joseph provided room and board until they could get on their feet. (Joe D'Anna.)

# *Five*

# SOCIETIES

The Fraternal Society of St. Joseph was formed on December 22, 1907, a few days after the first meeting at which community members gathered to discuss the building of Holy Family Church. The first president was Joseph Giurlanda, the vice president was Francesco Paolo D'Anna, and the secretary was Joseph Mazzola. Thirty men attended (most immigrants from Terrasini) and are now designated the first founders of the church. The group collected funds to build the church; on January 20, 1911, they became a mutual aid society, and they donated the first statue of St. Joseph on March 19, 1914. This photograph was taken in 1939 at the Feast of St. Joseph in the church basement. (Carl and Eleanora Bommarito.)

In 1945, the men of the parish gathered together for the Feast of St. Joseph in front of the first statue, which was blessed on March 19, 1914. They are, from left to right, (first row) unidentified, Ben Curcuru, and Tony D'Anna; (second row) unidentified, Sam Moceri, Angel ?, Tony Militello, and unidentified; (third row) unidentified, Buster Lucido, Domenic Corrado, unidentified, Jack Tocco, Seb Moceri, unidentified, Sam Buffa, Nick Moceri, and unidentified; (fourth row) two unidentified men, John Mercurio, Sam Licito, Bill Locricchio, Sam Misuraca, unidentified, Peter Vitale, and two unidentified men. (Rosary Amore.)

The St. Joseph Society of the Workers of Cinisi was founded on January 1, 1963, taking on the traditions of the First Fraternal Order of St. Joseph as members had died out. The founders of the new society were friends Casimiro DiMaggio, Natale Palazzolo, Antonino Palazzolo, and Salvatore Palazzolo. These men felt that immigrants of Cinisi, Sicily, should be united in an association. The purpose of the society was to preserve and transmit their religious roots, traditions, and customs for future generations, with the idea of working in honor of the patron St. Joseph. (Author's collection.)

The procession statue used today was given to the society 35 years ago by Mario and Nancy Viviani. They have been members of Holy Family for over 50 years. Mario and Nancy have owned and operated Michigan Artistic Creations for 56 years. Mario, an artist, molded and painted this statue of St. Joseph. (Author's collection.)

In 1955, Pope Pius XII instituted the feast day of St. Joseph the worker to coincide with international Labor Day and May Day. As Joseph labored as a carpenter to care for his family, the feast day celebrates the workingman. On the first Sunday in May of each year at Holy Family, a procession, mass, and feast celebrate and honor St. Joseph. Tony Badalamenti and his wife, Mimma, reenact the journey of Joseph and Mary into Egypt for the birth of Jesus Christ, when finally an innkeeper allows them to use his barn. Viva San Giuseppe! Then the feast begins, with food prepared by the women of the church. (Author's collection.)

Fr. John Stopponi leads the 1998 Feast Day procession around the Chrysler freeway with altar boys Domenic and Andrew Casinelli and Deacon Mike Jara. Now the residential neighborhoods are gone, the crowds are smaller, but the tradition continues. (Author's collection.)

In 1870, Pope Pius IX declared Joseph the patron saint of the universal church and promoted the "Patronage" feast day, to honor Joseph for the care of his wife, Mary, and their son, Jesus. St. Joseph's Day occurs on March 19, and at Holy Family it is usually celebrated on the Sunday closest to the 19th with a special mass and the blessing of bread. (Emmanuel Gravame.)

Some of the current members of the St. Joseph Society pictured here are Joe Biondo, Salvatore Palazzolo, Al Chirco, Vito Chirco, Filippo Leone, Cesara Manzella, Mimmo Palazzolo, president Tony Badalamenti, Tony Palazzolo, Sal Biondo, and Vincenzo Finazzo. (Tony Badalamenti.)

The Sanctuary of the Madonna del Ponte near Giancaldaia is pictured. The legend of Madonna del Ponte, the Blessed Mother of the Bridge, originated in the 14th century. An old man from Partinaco came across a small grotto near a bridge in Giancaldaia. A light was shining out from around a statue of the blessed mother and child within the grotto. No one believed the man's story except for the priest, who followed him back to the grotto. (Peter Ferro.)

When the pair attempted to move the statue her shoe fell off and made an imprint beneath. The priest saw a sign that they should move the statue up the hill. As the old man and the priest labored futilely, men from the neighboring towns—Alcamo, Balestate, and Trappeto—appeared, each with a similar story and a desire to carry the Madonna home. The road from Partinico to the church is pictured. (Peter Ferro.)

To prevent argument, the men agreed to put the statue on an ox cart and to let "her" decide where she wanted to go. In the middle of a nearby bridge, the oxen stopped and would not move. Eventually the men decided to leave the statue, naming her Blessed Mother of the Bridge. The four towns are united in shared belief. The church, located on the outskirts of Partinico, is pictured above. (Peter Ferro.)

The townspeople agreed to have a painting made of the Madonna, depicting what had happened on the bridge. The painting is kept in the Cathedral of Partinico, and each year, on the Sunday of Albis—the day devoted to divine mercy—it is paraded from the cathedral through the countryside to return to the church on the outskirts of Partinico, pictured here, the next Sunday. (Peter Ferro.)

The Società di Mutuo Soccorso Partinicese Maria SS. del Ponte was formed on August 19, 1928, and was incorporated on October 17, 1928. After 30 years the society became known as the Club Madonna del Ponte. Photographed here in the 1940s, society women participate in a parade, holding the first banner of Maria SS. del Ponte di Partinico. (Rose Marie Fessler.)

The Società di Mutuo Soccorso Partinicese Maria SS. del Ponte was formed to promote, support, and encourage interest in culture, education, and professions, and the efforts continue. From left to right, Tom Landa, Sam Ioco, Peter Ferro, and Emilio Torres are pictured here at a Madonna del Ponte fund-raising dinner in 2000. (Peter Ferro.)

The feast day of Madonna del Ponte is still celebrated each year at Holy Family on the Sunday following Easter. This year, the society dedicated to Madonna del Ponte will be celebrating its 80th anniversary. The Holy Family feast day statue is pictured here. (Peter Ferro.)

Joe Toia is president of Madonna del Ponte, secretary of the Italian Chamber of Commerce, and a former president of the Italian Bar Association. Toia was grand marshal of the 2007 Columbus Day parade. He is proud to continue the traditions that his fathers before him started hundreds of years ago in Sicily. Today he carries on the 80-year-old tradition of Madonna del Ponte at Holy Family Church. (Author's collection.)

St. Burgundafara, the noble virgin known as St. Fara, was born in the year 572. Her parents, Count Agnerico and Countess Leonegonda, pushed her to marry, but she remained faithful to Jesus. Each time Fara disobeyed, her parents punished her, and she became increasingly ill. Fara went blind and her father imprisoned her, but she endured these sufferings with holy resignation to the will of God. When God learned of Fara's suffering, he reprimanded her father, who repented and knelt at the feet of St. Eustasio, promising to accept her beliefs. Fara's dowry was used to build a monastery. (Joe Biondo.)

*Mrs. Rosolia (Vitale) Misuraca — Paolo Misuraca, First Presidente 1924.*

## History and Purpose
### of
## Societa Santa Fara Di Cinisi in Detroit

### —HISTORY—

The Society of Santa Fara of Cinisi was founded on April 10, 1924. By an inspiration of compassion and love to one cinisaro to another. The early emigrant cinisaro settled altogether in the area of Fort St. and St. Aubin, near the Holy Family church...As it is narrated by our oldest leaders members;...Mr. Vincenzo Finazzo and Mr. Paolo Misuraca on a sunny day of April, 1924. We were standing at the corner of Fort St. and St. Aubin when a funeral car (Carrozza Funebre) passed by with no one following the deceased (no accompaniment), no family, no friends. The two men asked...Who was the man that passed on? A passer by answered...Un cinisaro. Mr. Vincenzo Finazzo and Mr. Paolo Misuraca said: We must form a Societa' Di Santa Fara Protettrice Di Cinisi, to help and respect each other. They gathered with a group of close friends at the residence of Mr. Paolo Misuraca, 2218 Fort Street, Detroit, Michigan. The founders were: Paolo Misuraca, Vincenzo Finazzo, Paolo Lauricella, Rocco Palazzolo, Matteo Orlando.

The first president Paolo Misuraca, 1924...Second president Lauricella 1930. Third Vincenzo Finazzo, 1935...Fourth Rocco Palazzolo, 1938...Fifth, Andrea Cracchiolo...Sixth Rosolino Anania...Seventh Sam Misuraca (figlio di Paolo)...Eighth Jerry Vitale, 1982 & 1983...Ninth president, Andrea Biondo 1984 & 1985. Our societa' has been one of the greatest society in the community of Detroit, Mich. We, cinisara have a Societa' Di Santa Fara in Chicago, president Joe Salamone, in Brooklyn, president Carlo Lauricella...In St. Louis, president, no longer existing. The purpose of our society is to...Work in harmony with each other for the uplifting of the social, moral, educational and citizenship of the community, and to promote, support and encourage interest in culture, education and the professions.

This advertisement for the Società Santa Fara di Cinisi, devoted to St. Burgundafara, or St. Fara, appeared in 1985. (Joe Biondo.)

St. Fara died on December 7, 658, at the age of 86. Almost 1,000 years after St. Fara's death, men invaded France, devastating sacred places. The Benedictine nuns at St. Fara's monastery prayed for protection. As the nuns opened St. Fara's grave to find her body intact, a messenger arrived to announce that the enemy was almost destroyed. On the same day, a blind woman came to touch St. Fara and was cured of her afflictions. Since that time, St. Fara has granted favors to the blind, mute, and crippled. This statue was created and donated by artist Mario Viviani in 1998. (Author's collection.)

The Società Santa Fara di Cinisi in Detroit usually celebrates its feast day at Holy Family Church on the second Sunday in June with a procession of society members and parishioners. Photographed on a feast day in 1947, participants pictured here include Vincenzo Finazzo, Sam Misuraca, Casimiro DiMaggio, Salvatore Randazzo, Giuseppe Biondo, and Vincenzo Impastato. (Joe Biondo.)

In 1622, a man from Sicily who knew of the good graces of St. Fara came to want to paint her. He was unsure as to how to portray her, and while considering, a stranger handed a depiction of St. Fara: in one hand a staff of wheat; in the other, an open book; at her feet, a farmer sowing wheat, a farmer harvesting wheat, and a farmer bundling wheat. The man looked to thank the stranger, but he was gone. In 1662, a Benedictine nun found the painting and decided to build a chapel to St. Fara. The people of Cinisi did not have a church; they put the names of many saints into an urn and drew St. Fara's name. The Cinisesi built the church and named it for her. (Joe Biondo.)

Sam Misuraca, son of the first president of the Società Santa Fara di Cinisi Francesco Paolo, became the seventh president. In 1948, Sam and his wife, Mary Catalano, donated the statue of Santa Fara to Holy Family Church, which still stands there today. (Frank and Josephine Carta.)

On the feast day of 1949, the men of Santa Fara crowd the sidewalk in front of the church. Pictured are Antonio Iacoppel, Domenico Maransano, Vincenzo Finazzo, Francesco Biondo, Frank Palazzolo, Luigi Vitale, Joe Sclafani, Antonio Chirco, Vincenzo, Cassasi, Vincenzo Agrusa, Damiano Evola, Girolamo Evola, Salvatore Maltese, and Sam Misuraca. (Joe Biondo.)

In celebration of the 25th anniversary of the society at the feast of Santa Fara, Fr. Benedict Ferretti blesses the statue and Father Bonfil and Fr. Noel Patacconi assist in the mass and the unveiling of a new statue. The beautiful and caring Mary (Catalano) Misuraca was still alive and well in 2007 at 105 years of age. (Frank and Josephine Carta.)

Today the men of Santa Fara continue the traditions of their ancestors. They have hosted many fund-raising events over the years, and Holy Family Church has benefited countless times because of their extreme charity. (Joe Biondo.)

Sam Misuraca reigned as president of the Società Santa Fara di Cinisi for 36 years, after which the members decided to elect a new president every two years. Pictured from left to right are past and present presidents Damiano Evola (1998), Jerry Vitale (1982 and 1992), Anthony Chirco (1994), Al Chirco (2006), Joe Biondo (1996 and 2002), Michael Biondo (2004), and Andrea Biondo (1984). Not pictured are Salvatore Agrusa (1986), Giorgio Calabrese (1988), Paolo Orlando (1990), and Ben Palazzolo (2000). (Al Chirco.)

The people of Terrasini erected an altar in honor of the Madonna delle Grazie in the church. They ordered a statue to adorn the altar and which they would also use in processions. Bishop Foley told them that he would not allow them to carry the statue in procession, so they had it delivered to the home of Joseph Moceri, at 190 Hastings Street, where they hid it until the feast day. Joseph Moceri is pictured at left, as the king, in front of the church in 1912. (Joe D'Anna.)

The first procession of Madonna delle Grazie was held on September 8, 1912, for the feast of the nativity of Mary. The procession began at Joseph Moceri's, where the statue had been hidden due to controversy. There were bands, flags, and thousands of people crying out "Viva Maria." The procession took the long way to the church, and when they finally arrived, the bishop deemed to bless their statue, although he did not want her to go out again. The rest of the day was filled with food, music, and fireworks. (Emmanuel Gravame.)

The Palazzolo children prepare for the procession of Madonna delle Grazie in this photograph taken in 1933 on the front steps of their home on Alexandrine Street. Pictured left to right down the steps are Dominic, Frances, Rosalie, Carol, and Joanna. Their mother sewed the dresses and angel wings by hand. Both their father, Frank, and mother, Nynifa, were active in many of the clubs and societies and were founding members of Loggia Yolanda and the federation. All of the Palazzolo children were baptized in the parish. (Carol Palazzolo and Rosalie House.)

The statue of Madonna delle Grazie was cast from the original in the homeland—Terrasini, Sicily—as were several other statues in the church. Here two Holy Family men from Terrasini are pictured in the 1940s: Anthony Danna, dressed in military attire, and Nick Moceri, the tall handsome man to his right. (Rosary Amore)

The first advertisement for the Società di Mutuo Soccorso Madonna delle Grazie di Terrasini appeared in the *Italian Tribune* on February 11, 1911. The first president was Salvatore Brillati, and the secretary was Alessandro Cusumano.

The church courtyard was reworked in the 1960s. Most of the statues bear the names of members of Madonna delle Grazie; others were donated by other parishioners, some members of other societies. This photograph was taken soon after the completion of the renovated courtyard. Several Madonna delle Grazie members gather in front of a new statue; from left to right are Jenny Gallo, Bill Gietzen, Eleanora Bommarito, Fr. Benedict Ferretti, unidentified, Fr. Maurus Michelini, Tony D'Anna, and unidentified. (Carl and Eleanora Bommarito.)

The procession statue used today was purchased by Anthony and Frances D'Anna during a trip to Italy taken in the early 1950s. Pictured here from left to right are unidentified, Fr. Enzo Addari, Pietro Demoee, Vito Serra, Nino Tocco, Sal Manzella, and Mimmo D'Anna. (Author's collection.)

The feast day of Madonna delle Grazie is celebrated at Holy Family on the second Sunday of September with a grand procession and a mass. Today parishioners take great pride in continuing the traditions of their ancestors. Members of the society pictured are, from left to right, Vito Bommarito, Onifo Viviano, Jack Tocco Jr., Mike Aluia, Jack Tocco, Vito Serra, Steve Serra, Dr. Salvatore Ventimiglia, and Salvatore Ventimiglia. (Author's collection.)

Immigrants from Trapani, Sicily, brought their humble devotion to Maria S.S. di Trapani to Detroit. In 1935, three women were at the heart of the group: Maria Frontiera, Francesca Abbate, and Anna Todaro. United in their love of the Catholic religion and their Italian descent, the group adopted by-laws and created a religious banner, vowing to help their sisters in need. Their first procession in Detroit, in 1937, is pictured, with Maria Consiglio at top left. (Mary [Consiglio] Rosati.)

In 1936, the society had a statue of Maria S.S. di Trapani shipped to Detroit from Italy. It was blessed and dedicated in 1937, and the plaque at the altar reads, "Anthony D'Anna President, Maria di Mercurio, Vice President, Frank Abbate, Secretary, Dave Manardo, Giovanna Falsone, Maria Spagnuolo, Anna Giacalone, Frank Bagnasco, Baldassare Aloia, Anna Todaro, Frances D'Anna, Rosa Campo and Teresa Pace Council." During weddings it is tradition to give this Madonna of their homeland an offering of prayer and flowers, as do Ciro Poma and Giovanna Pace, photographed here. (Giovanna Poma.)

The women celebrated Maria S.S. di Trapani each year on August 16 with a mass and procession, lead by devotees carrying a replica of the original statue as well as their religious banner. The first banner was made in 1936. The banner used today was donated by Mr. and Mrs. Donato Patipilo in 1953 and was restored by Vincea Amaro and wife Josephine in 1995. The first president of the society was Maria Frontiera, who held meetings and began holding a dinner dance as a fund-raising event. To show solidarity, the sisters, pictured here in the 1940s, dressed in white. (Rose Marie Fessler.)

Maria Spagnuolo was a founding member of Maria S.S. di Trapani. Living to age 99, Spagnuolo was a member for 75 years and was also the leader for many years. Spagnuolo also cared for the church linens, taking them home by bus. When she was no longer able to continue her duties, her good friend and fellow member Maria Anna Pulizzi assumed the duties of the leader and organized the group's events. In 2003, they merged under the direction of the Conca D'Oro Club. (Elizabeth Falsone.)

In 1987, the Conca D'Oro Club, a social club whose members are mostly from cities and towns around Trapani, adopted Maria S.S. di Trapani as its patroness. The Conca D'Oro Club still celebrates every year with the help of Maria Sugameli. Pictured from left to right are Joe diSanto, president of the Conca D'Oro Club; Andy and Maria Sugameli, who was the society chairwomen; and Vince and Josephine Armero with other devotees behind them. (Maria Sugameli.)

Legend says that the statue was the property of a knight named Guerreggio. Returning from the Holy Crusades to his home in Pisa, Guerreggio transported the statue in a case. Guerreggio's ship suffered during violent storms, and the crew vowed to the Madonna to leave the statue on the first Christian land they came to. They landed in Trapani and the statue was taken to the church of Santa Maria del Parto. The statue was to be returned to Guerreggio, but each attempt failed. The bulls pulling the wagon meant to transport the statue to port went toward the outskirts of the city. It was understood that the Madonna wanted the statue to stay. The bulls stopped in front of the church of the Annunciation, where Carmelite monks received the statue in procession. (Maria Sugameli.)

Guerreggio agreed to donate it to the Trapanese, and the Madonna is still guarded at what is now known as the Basilica dell'Annunziata. After much devotion to the image, the statue became venerated with the title of Maria S.S. di Trapani. The graces invoked by the intercession of her image convinced the Carmelite monks to ask the Vatican for approval to give the statue a golden crown. Their request was approved, and in 1734, a crown was commissioned. The celebration was the first of its kind in Sicily. Golden keys hang from the statue's right arm to signify that she is the patron of the city of Trapani. (Maria Sugameli.)

The story of the statue began in the 13th century, when Carmelite friars escaped Mount Carmel and traveled to Trapani. According to documents, a notary by the name of Ribaldo donated his property to the Carmelite monks who established their community in Campagna, dedicating their church and convent to the Annunciation. One of the first graduates became a renowned saint, St. Alberto degli Abati. Water that has touched his relics has been known to cure fevers and other infirmities. (Maria Sugameli.)

Until a few decades ago, the statue of the Madonna was dressed in jewels and gold donated by those who had been healed by the Blessed Mother's intercession. The dress and donations are now conserved in the basilica's museum. (Maria Sugameli.)

*Maria Santissima* di Trapani

*Infonde sentimenti di fede, di luce e di speranza tanto da far esclamare*
*"CHI VUOL VEDERLA PIÙ BELLA VADA IN PARADISO!".*

The image of Maria S.S. Trapani has been in procession more than 20 times in the course of centuries; the first transport is said to have taken place in 1476, and the last in 1954. During the early processions, the image was carried and surrounded by hundreds of barefoot fishermen dressed in white garb. At the port in Trapani there is a replica of the statue peering out to sea. (Maria Sugameli.)

The veneration of the Blessed Mother of Trapani still is as strong as in years past. The devotion of Maria S.S. di Trapani is known as far as India. In Italy, pilgrims travel long distances on foot to celebrate the feast on August 16. Some devotees begin the celebration with a *quindicina*, visiting the basilica for 15 days leading up to the feast day, in thanksgiving and prayer for the Blessed Mother's intercession. In Detroit, devotees have celebrated with a procession since 1935. Leading this procession are Enza DiGrazia and Paoline Basilico. (Maria Sugameli.)

Alessandro Ciaramitaro was the first president of the Società di Mutuo Soccorso Monte S. Giuliano; his secretary was Antonio La Rocco. The society was approved for charter in August 1909, and it received approval in December of the same year. It operated out of 221 Macomb Street. The society was formed to help the sick and bury the dead of any Italian in need. (Emmanuel Gravame.)

The Società di Mutuo Soccorso Maria S.S. Dei
Miracoli of Alcamo was started in May 1912.
Each member was to pay $1 per month toward
their fund; in return, they would have a doctor
if needed and after six months seniority their
family would get help toward their funeral in
case of death. (DiMaggio family.)

Francesco Carta and his wife, Rosalia Mirabella, were original founders of the parish and of
the Alcomese Society. Carta was the first president of the society, and his good friend Pietro
Bellanca was the secretary. In 1940, Carta and Bellanca wrote a book on the history of the
church and of the statue of Alcamo; it was later translated into English by Joseph Paradise.
Without this record, the stories of many of the original founders would have been lost to time.
(Frank and Josephine Carta.)

There were several scandals around the statue of Maria S.S. Dei Miracoli. There were so few Alcamesi that it was hard to finance a statue; however, they started the venture in 1912. In 1916, the society procured a simple, inexpensive sculpture. Sculptor Alfonso Moroder charged only $360 for his work. By the time the Alcamesi added brass and lights and other items needed to celebrate the day of her arrival, it ended up costing $846 in total and they could not get her blessed by the bishop until 1918. In 1936, Francesco Carta's son Leo repainted the Madonna brilliant colors. (Author's collection.)

Fr. Benedict Ferretti is pictured here with some members of the Holy Face Society. Seen here are Serafina Asta (left), Jenny Gallo (third from right), and Josephine Moceri (right). Today the Holy Face Society still exists but holds its devotions only once a year. (Carl and Eleanora Bommarito.)

*Six*

# CLUBS AND TRADITIONS

The M. Militello and J. Badalamenti American Legion Holy Family Post 570 was established in 1948. At the first meeting, in order to name the post, the group chose five names of compadri who had been killed in the war, put the names into a hat, and drew two. The first was Michael Militello and the second, Joseph Badalamenti, who is pictured here. Badalamenti died in service to his country in Normandy in 1945. (Post 570.)

One of the original founders of the Holy Family Post 570, Peter Paul Tocco is still a healthy and active member in 2007 at age 93. Tocco's parents left Terrasini, Sicily, in the early 1900s and settled in Detroit when he was five years old. Tocco was drafted into the army in 1941 and was honorably discharged at the end of World War II. He was the fifth commander of Post 570 and was instrumental in getting a papal blessing from Pope John Paul II. Post 570 is the only American Legion Post to have such an honor. (Peter Paul Tocco.)

Post 570's first Veterans Day parade was photographed in 1948. The celebration included the christening of the flags and a mass at Holy Family, officiated by Fr. Benedict Ferretti. Paul Giordano, first commander, leads the parade, and Salvatore Corrado holds the American flag as they proceed down Fort Street. On April 18, 1949, the members of Post 570 received their temporary charter, and by 1951 they had received their permanent charter. (Post 570.)

Members of Post 570 are pictured at their first dinner banquet in 1949 at the Fort Shelby hotel. From left to right are Mike Frontera; unidentified; Carl Bommarito; John Pellerito, fourth commander; Paul Giordano, first commander; unidentified; Tony Bagnasco, second commander; Peter Paul Tocco, fifth commander; unidentified; Frank Belvedere; John Ruggero; and Anthony Lafata, seventh commander. (Post 570.)

Around 1954, the post members moved their headquarters from Holy Family Church into a building at 11326 Whittier Street on Detroit's east side. Father Ferretti was the designated chaplain and was there to bless the flags and new building. (Post 570.)

Giovanni Lafata, eighth commander of the Holy Family American Legion Post 570, is pictured here during his tour of duty in the U.S. Army in Scotland during World War II. Lafata was an active member of Post 570 for more than 30 years. (Peter Paul Tocco.)

In 1955, the women of the Post 570 members received a letter inviting them to join the Ladies Auxiliary of the American Legion. Lucy Kittendorf (left) was installed as president at their first meeting; Josephine Lafata was vice president; Mary Genovese was secretary; and her sister Jenny Catalfio was historian. The women raised funds for veterans, organized events, and spoke in schools about the flag and patriotism. (Post 570.)

Pictured at the 2007 Holy Family Post 570 annual picnic are Joseph and Frances Rubello, Bonnie Leone, Sarah and Mel Morrone, Grace Tocco, Annette and Izzy Cipriano, Peter Paul Tocco, Tony Ciaramitaro, Ed Mangold, Larry Kelly, Rina and Joe Provanzano, Joe Maniaci, Ciro Taormina, and Stephanie Ciaramitaro. The wives no longer have their own auxiliary club, but they still get involved. (Author's collection.)

Post 570 still boasts one of the largest memberships of any American Legion post in Michigan. A few of today's members are pictured; from left to right are (first row) Angelo Miele Commander, Joe Bonno, Cy Taormina, Pat Presti, and Ed Mangold; (second row) Mel Morrone, Tony Ciaramitaro, Peter Tocco, Joseph Provanzano, Joe Prano, John Marino, unidentified, Tony Maisano, Izzy Cipriano, Sam D'Anna, and Joe Rubello. (Author's collection.)

Once called the Club of Loggia Principessa Iolandana, this social club for women is now known as Loggia Yolanda No. 37. Formed on May 15, 1932, some of the first founders were Rose Mangiapane, Mary Bocca, Ninfa Palazzolo, Rose Cilluffo, Kathrine D'Anna, Serafina Asta, Angelina Anania, and Ida Perrone. This group, along with many other Sicilian societies, belonged to the Federazione Siciliana Delagation of Michigan. (Rose Marie Fessler.)

The original members of Loggia Principessa stand in front of the church in 1932. Identified here are Maria Perrone, Mrs. Peter Asta, Ida Perrone, Mary Calcagno, Ninfa Palazzolo, Serafina Asta, Mrs. Losardo, Anna Perrone, Vita Licari, and Mrs. Filppono. Today the society has 74 members, and its president and secretary are Rose Marie Fessler and Gena Mangiapane, respectively. (Rose Marie Fessler.)

For many years the society of Loggia Principessa Ilonda was in charge of the queens' courts for all of the societies and for the final Columbus Day pageant. Today the societies each sponsor their own pageant and then send their winner to the Columbus Committee's final pageant. Pictured in the 1930s are Marianna Perrone (far left, front), Frances Palazzolo (far right, front), Angie Padino (just behind Palazzolo), and Ralph Mancini. (Rose Marie Fessler.)

The children of Holy Family led a Fourth of July parade in the 1930s with various Sicilian and Italian societies participating. Alfonso Pizzamenti plays piccolo. (Rose Marie Fessler.)

In 1909, Italians and Sicilians formed a committee to have a statue made of Christopher Columbus. The *Italian Tribune*, which had started publication that year, spearheaded the effort. On Columbus Day 1910, the statue was unveiled in its place on Washington Boulevard. This photograph captures a Columbus Day celebration in the 1950s. (Rose Marie Fessler.)

This photograph was taken on Columbus Day 2007. Every year after the mass and reception at the church a wreath is placed at the statue of Columbus. Pictured are Leonardo Maniaci of Santa Fara; Russ Loduca, president of the Downriver Sicilia Club; Dino Valle, radio announcer; Al Chirco, president of Santa Fara; Mike Chirco, "Man of the Year"; Dominic LaRosa, master of ceremonies; Al Zaccaro, "Humanitarian of the Year"; and Sam Genovese, president of the Montelepre Club. (Author's collection.)

In 2007, Club Madonna del Ponte's queen, Lauren Hilliker, won the Columbus Day pageant. Hilliker, a high school senior and member of the National Honor Society with perfect attendance for 11 of her 12 years in school, was a straight A student and received awards in math and science. Hilliker, who works for a real estate company, takes pride in her Italian heritage and traditions. The first runner up was Kristi Muscatello, second was Georgette Aneed, and third was Anna Maria Tucci. (Author's collection.)

Frances Perrone, Miss Columbus Day 1963, is pictured here at Cobo Hall with Pres. Lyndon B. Johnson and his wife Lady Byrd Johnson after the Columbus Day dinner. (Frances Perrone.)

The Columbian Federation of America
CONVENTION
BELLE ISLE CASINO · DETROIT, MICHIGAN
SEPT. 10, 1946

WELCOME TO DETROIT
DELEGATES OF THE
COLUMBIAN FEDERATION

Between 1946 and 1954, the Loggia Statale del Michigan of the Columbian Federation of Italian American Societies organized and sponsored the events for the Columbus Day celebration. The group meets nationally every four years. In the 1950s, the Federazione Siciliana Delagation of Detroit hosted the convention for delegates from the state of Michigan. Some of the members pictured here are Mike Zito, Peter Asta, Ben Ajello, Ninfa Palazzolo, Bill Mangiapane, Angelina Poma, Tom Asta, and Frank Palazzolo. (Rose Marie Fessler.)

Lodge Figli della Sicilia No. 227 Columbian Federation, was founded on February 10, 1936. Some of the members of today's club are pictured; from left to right are Roy Cracchio, Vito Giambanco, Walter Borla (Columbian Federation national president), Sebastiano Previti, Salvatore Preveti (Lodge Figli della Sicilia president), Joseph Grammatico, and Giuseppe Cottone. (Sebastiano Previti.)

Over the years, many have served as ushers at Holy Family Church. The 2007 Ushers Club is pictured; from left to right are Keith Morrone, Benedetto Morrone, Thomas Neil, William Leone, Lee BeGole, Mel Morrone, and Sam Scalisi. Tony and Mario Viviani are not pictured. (Author's collection.)

La Festa degli Schietti takes place on Easter Sunday. The tradition is traced back to the 1860s in Terrasini. The event starts on Saturday morning with the tree cutting. It is then decorated with colored ribbon and bells. The challenge is to balance an orange tree on the palms of their hand, held over their head. (Sam Genovese.)

On Sunday morning after the mass the priest blesses the trees. The bachelors stake the trees in front of the houses of their fiancées to win them over. In the afternoon, the festival continues with a reward for the man who can hold his tree aloft for the longest duration. This feast was still celebrated at Holy Family until only a few years ago. (Rose Patchett.)

Chiesa Cattolica Maria Santissima delle Grazie (Madonna delle Grazie) is the church of the ancestors of Terrasini, Sicily. To the right on the church is St. Joseph; to the left, St. Peter; and in the center, Madonna delle Grazie. All of the statues at Holy Family are modeled after the ones here. The census records of Terrasini start in 1684, and parish records go back to 1736. It is said that the first shrine was built to the Madonna in 1583. People traveling to Trapani stopped in Terrasini to rest and eventually started settling there. (Author's collection.)

In 1960, Sam Genovese and his new bride, Francesca Gaglio, were photographed sitting in a traditional wedding cart in Sicily. (Sam Genovese.)

The Terrasini Club was formed in 1977. Using the Ambassador Bridge as their symbol, the members have built a bridge between Detroit and their ancestors' homeland. Fr. John Stopponi (third from right) is pictured blessing the orange tree with Mike Aluia (second from left) and Vito Serra (second from right). (Author's collection.)

Bachelors gather at the Italian Cultural Center for La Festa degli Schietti. Along with Terrasini, this club is the only in Michigan to hold the traditional competition. Here Vito Serra shows his strength. (Sam Genovese.)

Tradition continues, rain or shine. In 2007, Maria Sugameli was photographed gathering children to carry the rosary for the procession of Madonna di Trapani. Andrew Biondo, Giovanni, Antonio, and Alfonso Moceri, pictured from left to right, are excited to be a part of the feast day. (Maria Sugameli.)

Rosario Gaglio is pictured here in the procession of Società SS. Crocifisso di Montelepre. Gaglio was a founder and one of the longest-standing members of the society, living to age 93. Today Gaglio's grandson Roy is the president of the society. Gaglio was also involved with the Santa Rosalia Society, and he donated the original brass candlesticks for the Holy Family altar. Gaglio walked to the church from Gratiot Avenue weekly. (Antonia Valentine.)

Società SS. Crocifisso di Montelepre celebrates the holy crucifix, the symbol of the Lord, who suffered because he loved everyone. The symbol of the crucified Christ is a comfort to all. This society procession took place in the 1930s. (Antonia Valentine.)

Serafina Serra crowns the statue of the Blessed Mother in the Holy Family courtyard. Her sister Lena looks up from below while Rose Cilluffo leads the hymns. (Sara Scrivano.)

In the May crowning of 1971, Mariella Viviani (left) and Eileen Topolewski had the honor of crowning the Madonna, while Grace Capizzo led the hymns. These three girls took all of their sacraments at Holy Family. (Sara Scrivano.)

Fr. Bonfil Bottazzo is pictured with the first communion class of 1981. (Beverly Bleggi.)

Children once filled the choir loft of Holy Family for special occasions. Today only adults play this role. Joseph Amicangelo, pictured here, has performed in the choir and has acted as director for more than 50 years. Today the organist is Judy Johnson. (Joe Amicangelo.)

This Holy Family Young Men's Club, was founded in the late 1930s. Most of the members had gone to war and had married and begun families shortly after returning home. As these men matured, membership dwindled, and the club reformed as American Legion Post 570. Identified here are John and Lucy Pellerito, Bill Leto, Grace Leto, Peter Tocco, Charlie Gelardi, Angie Leto, Edith Gelardi, Tom and Rose Moceri, Tony Leto, Tony Ciaramitaro, Babe and Andy Vermiglio, Annette and Peter Tocco, Mike Pulizzi, John Cusmano, Larry Leto, Pearl Bagnasco, and Catherine and Tony Bagnasco. (Peter, Paul, and Grace [Leto] Tocco.)

The first organ powered by a turning crank appeared in the 1700s. This Sicilian immigrant, identified only as Giuseppe, was lucky to have $100—enough to buy a monkey and an organ—which allowed him to make a living for his family. Giuseppe walked around the neighborhood of Holy Family playing his organ. His monkey danced and collected coins from the children who gathered. People loved Giuseppe, who also carried news and gossip throughout the neighborhood. (Author's collection.)

The Neapolitan Serenaders have been playing wonderful Italian songs for parties and feast day celebrations at Holy Family for many years. (Author's collection.)

Emanuele Gravame was born in 1873 in Taranto, Italy, and came to the United States in 1905. This photograph was taken around 1920. Gravame was a member of the Società di Mutuo Soccorso Dante Alighieri, which had started in 1908 and held meetings at Rivard and Sherman Streets. Gravame and his son Carmelo were founding members and helped collect money to build and erect the statue of Dante Alighieri, which still resides on Belle Isle today. (Emmanuel Gravame.)

For many years Holy Family held catechism classes for levels from preschool through 12th grade, operating out of the University of Detroit Jesuit. Pictured are principal Pat Leonard and teachers Mrs. Fournier, Mrs. James, Mrs. Topolewski, Mrs. Voytush, and Mrs. Groves, along with one of the seminarians, Mr. Sobolewski. (Beverly Bleggi.)

Mario (left) and Tony Viviani are seen here in the ceremony marking the disposition of Cristo Morto. This tradition originated in Italy and is still carried out on Good Friday at Holy Family. Mario and his family have undertaken this honorable tradition for more than 50 years. (Author's collection.)

These dedicated women gave their time and patience to teach children the word of God, the virtue of good will, and many other lessons. Pictured from left to right are Jean Lendway, Beverly Bleggi, Val Rizzardi, and Mrs. Groves. (Beverly Bleggi.)

Parishioners Bill Leone (left) and Dr. Charles Pearson (right) carry the body of Christ during the Cristo Morto ceremony. A statue embodying Our Lady of Sorrows follows immediately behind in the candlelight procession around the church. (Author's collection.)

In 1912, the societies of St. Joseph, Madonna delle Grazie, St. Peter, and St. Vincent DePaul wanted to build a school and hall adjacent to the church; Bishop John Foley would not allow it. They agreed to fund the enlargement and finishing of the basement if the bishop would allow them to use the hall, as well as to sublet the hall to other parties. The societies agreed to never use the hall for irreligious or immoral purposes. In the 1930s, children often put on plays. Pictured here are Rose and Sam Bommarito, Margaret Garazzo, the Rubino children, Fannie Pellerito, and Frances Moceri. (Carl and Eleanora Bommarito.)

Tradition continues. The children of Holy Family parishioners put on the annual Christmas play, directed and narrated by Karleen Viviani. After the play the children sing happy birthday to Jesus and have a luncheon with Santa. This annual event is organized by Josephine DeMaria to raise money to cover winter heating expenses, which sometimes exceed $2,000 a month. (Author's collection.)

# *Seven*

# SACRAMENTS

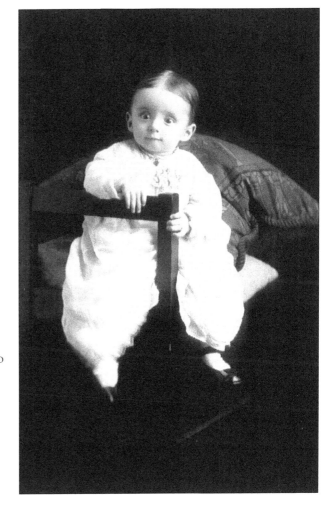

Antonio Tedesco, whose grandfather was one of the founding members of the parish, was the only child of Joachim Tedesco and Bella May McMaster. Baptized in 1912 by Fr. Aloysius Luigi Parodi, Antonio also took his first communion at Holy Family and was confirmed at the church. Antonio married Irene DeVreese, and they had two daughters. Antonio held four patents in the United States for inventions relevant to the automotive industry. (Sandra [Tedesco] Smith.)

Son of Vito Tocco and Rosalia Zerilli, Giacomo "Jack" Tocco was baptized and took first communion at Holy Family Church. Jack graduated from the University of Detroit in 1949 with a bachelor's of science degree. This handsome young man married Maria Meli in 1952, and all eight of their children were baptized at Holy Family. Jack has been involved with Holy Family Church, Madonna delle Grazie, the Terrasini Club, and the St. Louis Center for many years. His charity and his loyalty to his Sicilian roots and church will never be forgotten. Jack Tocco is on the Holy Family Church centennial committee. (Jack Tocco.)

ROSALIA ZERILLI
N. 16 DIC. 1870
M. 1 OTT. 1931

Rose (Tocco) Zerilli, the beloved and respected wife of Anthony Zerilli, died at the age of 61 on October 1, 1931. Her funeral was one of the largest that had been held in metropolitan Detroit. Over 480 flower arrangements filled the house and covered the lawn; four truckloads of flowers were dropped from an airplane, which circled over the home and the mile-long procession to Holy Family. Father Alberic Maggiore chanted a solemn High Mass, and the service was so crowded that some people had to sit in the basement and outside of the church. (Author's collection.)

Joseph Zerilli, son of Antonio Zerilli and Rose Tocco, married Joanna Finazzo on April 26, 1922. Joanna was the daughter of Joseph Finazzo and Josephine Corrado, both born in Terrasini. The Finazzos first lived at 2259 Congress Street. Joseph went into partnership with his cousin Vito Tocco, and together they owned many successful businesses. One of the first was Pfeiffer Brewing Company; they also owned a car dealership, a bakery, and a linen service. Holy Family has benefited greatly from their charity. All of their Zerilli children were baptized in the church. (Greg Cipriano.)

Over 400 mourners paid their final respects to Joseph Zerilli. Zerilli died October 30, 1977, in Bon Secours Hospital at the age of 79 after being ill for several months. He was laid in state at Bagnasco's Funeral Home in the Rolls Royce of caskets, which was copper, with his head upon a gray pleated velvet pillow, while sprays of long-stemmed roses decorated the back and lower portion of the casket. Former pastor of the church and longtime friend of the Zerilli family, Fr. Benedict Ferretti came back to officiate in the funeral services along with four other priests; there were over 400 mourners and the procession down Jefferson Avenue stretched over a mile. The media failed to mention the loyalty of this parishioner who came to church every Sunday until his health prevented him from doing so. (Author's collection.)

Joseph Maniaci, son of Isadore Maniaci and Pauline Bommarito, was baptized and confirmed at Holy Family. He grew up working in his father's produce business until he went into the army in 1943. When he returned home he went into advertising for awhile and married Mary O'Donnell and raised three girls and a boy, a girl and a boy of which were twins. He worked for Beauty Craft Supply for 38 years and was married one month short of 50 years when his dear wife, Mary, died. Joe has early memories of Holy Family and Fr. John Vismara and thinks of the parish as his second home. He has also been a member of Madonna delle Grazie and Post 570 for many years. (Joe Maniaci.)

Vito Giacalone, the son of Giacomo Giacalone and Antonia Ciaramitaro, was baptized at Holy Family. He married Stella Rose in 1948. The Giacalone family has had several generations make their sacraments in the church, and they have been strong financial supporters on several restoration projects. (Maria Lamia.)

Vito "Bill" Tocco was a part of the first generation of men that supported and protected the parish of Holy Family. He died on May 28, 1972, at the age of 74, of heart failure at Bon Secours Hospital. His body laid in state at Bagnasco Funeral Home on Harper Avenue in St. Clair Shores in a beautiful mahogany casket. Mourners came to Holy Family to pay their last respects but had to quickly rush into the church as photographers snapped pictures of the luxury cars that were triple-parked around the streets of the church. This handsome, successful, and generous parishioner was a true devout Catholic that took his sacraments seriously. (Author's collection.)

Vita Guastella, having all of her sacraments from Holy Family, was the daughter of Gaetano Guastella and Josephine Salerno, who were among the first parishioners. Vita was baptized by Father Parodi on November 8, 1914, and she lived to be 93 years old. (Joann Frederick.)

Giuseppe Tadaro, born in Sicily in 1902, was the son of Giuseppe Tadaro and Giovanna Curso. He was living at 2148 Helen Street in Detroit, when he proposed marriage to Vita Guastella in 1941. They had three children, Josephine, Joseph and Giovanna, who were twins. Vita had a great love for Holy Family Church. (Joann Frederick.)

In 1915, Alessandro Ciaramitaro and his wife, Pauline LaRosa, are pictured with their family on the day of their third child Francesco's baptism and daughter Josephine's first communion with their son John. Their daughter Josephine was born in January 1909 and was not baptized until her brother John's birth in March 1911. At the age of 99, she is the oldest known living person baptized to the parish and in the church of Holy Family. (Emmanuel Gravame.)

Early parishioners Rosaria Stellino and Salvatore Scalisi, both from Alcamo in the province of Trapani, were married at Holy Family in 1917 by Fr. Giovanni Boschi. Today their grandson Sam Scalisi has been a parishioner for over 50 years. He still carries on the traditions and maintains the church that they were so proud of being a part of. (Sam Scalisi.)

Salvatore "Sam" DiMaggio, born on East Lafayette Street, was a faithful parishioner baptized and confirmed at Holy Family. Sam started working at the age of 14 selling newspapers on street corners for the *Detroit Times* and later became a regular employee where he stayed until they closed in 1960, after which he started his own fence company. He married his childhood sweetheart, Angie Maniaci. Angie was a kind and loving person who retired from Dodge after 30-plus years. They had desperately wanted to start a family, but could not, so instead Sam and Angie treated everyone else's children as their own, making many families very happy over the years. (DiMaggio family.)

The oldest known living couple married at Holy Family, Albert Fontana, the son of Vincenzo Fontana and Gigeria Marrone, married Mary Fanfalone, the daughter of Gaspare Fanfalone and Rosalia Virgilio. They were married 65 years ago by Fr. Benedict Ferretti on July 25, 1942. Late for the reception that day, they almost did not make it when a police officer pulled all of the wedding cars over on the way and gave them tickets for honking their horns. (Albert and Mary Fontana.)

One of the first parishioners to Holy Family, Alfonso Pizzimenti was born in Terrasini, Sicily, in 1891, the son of Dominic and Rosalia Lopiccolo. He was married on January 25, 1916, to Angelina Viviano, the daughter of Joseph Viviano and Gratia Tocco, who were also from Terrasini. He started out with a small produce business to provide for his growing family, the children of which were all baptized in the church. They were also one of the first members of Madonna delle Grazie. Their grandson Fr. Eduard Perrone is now one of the most beloved priests in the archdiocese in the city of Detroit. (Grace Perrone.)

La S. V. é invitata a voler
intervire al matrimonio del
*Signor Giuseppe Bono*
con la
*Signorina Caterina Finazzo*
che avrá luogo
Sabato, 20 Luglio 1929
ore 9 a. m.
*Chiesa della Sacra Famiglia*
angolo di Fort e Hastings Sts.
Ricevimento all' Amity Temple
9375 Amity Ave., angolo di Parkview.

Residenza della Sposa: 2924 E. Fort
Futura residenza: 2924 E. Fort
Detroit, Mich.

This is the wedding invitation of the parents of Charlie Bono, who were longtime parishioners and good friends of the Benedictine priests. (Charles Bono.)

Vincenzo Cusmano, born in Terrasini in 1894, was the son of Salvatore Cusmano and Antonia Palazzolo. He married Vita Cracchiolo, the daughter of Joseph Cracchiolo and Concetta Palazzolo. She was born in Detroit in 1902, and her family was one of the first parishioners of the church. They married on April 26, 1919. (Concetta Alesiak.)

Msgr. Peter Lentine was baptized on May 25, 1919, at Holy Family Church. His parents, Manuel Lentine and Josephine Randazzo, came to the United States in the early 1900s from Carini in the Province of Palermo. His father was in the produce business and worked hard, long hours to support his family so his children could have a better life. Father Lentine attended seminary school in Baltimore and Sacred Heart Seminary in Detroit. He was ordained a priest on May 20, 1950, by Cardinal Mooney at Blessed Sacrament. He has serviced the parishes of St. Elizabeth in Wyandotte, Assumption Grotto, St. Matthew's, and St. Rita all in Detroit. He has been the pastor at St. Philomena for the last 41 years. Monsignor Lentine is kind, caring, and respectful of others. He is proud of his Sicilian roots and admired by those who know him. (Fr. Peter Lentine.)

In the 1950s, Sam and Dannie Fanfalone had their children Michael and Rosalia baptized the same day by Fr. Joseph Muzzin. Pictured with the children are their godparents Bill Fanfalone, Mary Fontana, Doris Balsamo, and Albert Fontana. Both couples and the parents and children were all married at Holy Family. (Doris Fanfalone.)

Joseph Locricchio was born in 1917 to Vincenzo Locricchio and Josephine Bommarito. Like many of the families, they boarded at 190 Hastings Street with Joseph Moceri's family until they could get settled, and they were also his godparents. Joseph married Lena Aluia at Holy Family in 1943. (Lena Locricchio.)

Anthony Munaco was the first generation in his family to come to Detroit from Cinisi, Sicily. He married Petrina Zerilli, who was born in Detroit and whose parents were from Terrasini, Sicily. She was the daughter of one of the original founders of the church, Salvatore Zerilli, who was among one of the first 30 men to establish the parish in 1908.The Munaco family now has had four generations married at Holy Family Church. (Fran Marie Silveri.)

Anthony Munaco and Frances Viviano, both baptized at Holy Family Church, were married in 1952. (Fran Marie Silveri.)

Carl Munaco and Josephine Chirco married in 1981. (Fran Marie Silveri.)

Fran Marie Munaco and Richard Silveri married in 2006. (Fran Marie Silveri.)

Proud parents Bob and Sara (Cilluffo) Scrivano are seen here. Sara was the daughter of one of the Parisi eight. Bob and Sara's set of twins, Ann and Aileen, along with their two boys David and Michael, were the third generation in this family to have been baptized at Holy Family. From left to right are Bob, godparents John Cilluffo and Lina Serra, Fr. Bonfil Bottazzo, godparents Tom Fessler and Sarah Cilluffo, and Sarah. (Sara Scrivano.)

Peter Paul Tocco and Grace Leto, now the second oldest known living couple of the parish, married in 1946. They had five children together, and after the service Peter provided produce to the Detroit Board of Education for over 25 years from his warehouse in the eastern market. Over the years they have both been very active members of some of the clubs and societies of Holy Family. (Peter Paul Tocco.)

Sacraments continue at Holy Family as Samantha Dunlap makes her first communion. After 99 years as a parish, she also received the honor of crowning the Blessed Mother in the church for the May crowning while her proud parents, family, and parishioners looked on. The altar servers were Keith Morrone, Nicolas Delgato, Marcelo Alvarado, John Pearson, Antonio Morrone, and Anthony Potts. (Author's collection.)

Carrying on tradition, Bill Leone and Bonnie VanDerziel were married at Holy Family Church on Detroit's 300th birthday, in 2001, with a reception of 300 people. East meets west at the corner of Warren and Woodward Avenues where the reception hall of St. Paul catered to both families as the westsiders did not want to go east and the eastsiders did not want to go west. Guests ate every Italian food imaginable. They were entertained by Italian Strollers, Dean Martin, Frank Sinatra, and Elvis Presley impersonators. From left to right are Providence (Leone) Manney, Bill Leone, Bonnie VanDerziel, Melissa Paalanen, and Mike Hill (standing). (Author's collection.)

Fr. Anthony Bologna was baptized at Holy Family in 1918 by Father Parodi. He was the son of Dominic Bologna and Maria Garofalo, who lived on 365 Catherine Street. He attended Sacred Heart Seminary, and at the age of 22 he was ordained a priest and became part of the Archdiocese of Detroit. He was at several parishes in Detroit, including four that serviced the Italians and a couple in Dearborn. (Grace Corrollo.)

Early parishioners Dominic Bologna, son of Vincenzo Bologna and Gratia Palazzolo of Terrasini, married Maria Garofalo, the daughter of Antonio Garofalo and Catharina Pelisi, at Holy Family Church on September 2, 1914. They had several children, all of which were baptized at the church. Their son Anthony went on to become a priest. (Grace Corrollo.)

This photograph captures the perfect lineup for a perfect day, with the women of the church present in a traditional show of solidarity on the occasion of the wedding of Jack Gaglio and Rose Siagursa, married in 1937. (Antonina Valentine.)

In 1955, a crowd cheers and throws rice for the happy couple, Luke Vitale and Angie Lunardo. Today at Holy Family and many other churches the custom of throwing rice is no longer permitted. (Angie Vitale.)

Vito Tocco, son of Giacomo Tocco and Nicolina Moceri, married Rosalia Zerilli, daughter of Antonio Zerilli and Rosalia Tocco, in the church on September 26, 1923. Vito came to the United States in 1910 from Terrasini, Sicily, when he was 13 years old. Vito became a citizen after serving in the army during World War I and became a successful businessman; he was one of the first men to join the newly built Holy Family Church. Vito and Rose raised five daughters and two sons, all of whom were baptized at Holy Family. Pictured from left to right are (first row) unidentified, Lena Tocco, father of the bride Antonio Zerilli, Vito Tocco, Rosalia Zerilli, mother of the bride Rose (Tocco) Zerilli, Josephine Zerilli, and unidentified; (second row) Rose and Sam Serra, Joseph Tocco, Stephanie Tocco, Serafina Zerilli, Joe Zerilli, and unidentified; (third row) Jack Tocco, Zina Morocco, Josephine and Massi Zito, Paul Moceri, Sam Tocco, Russell and Grace Cutino, and Caesar Laura. (Jack Tocco.)

# *Eight*

# PAST AND PRESENT

Vito Leone and his new bride, Provvidenza Pagano, left Terrasini via Palermo, sailing on the S.S. *Patria* and arriving at Ellis Island on November 1, 1922. They took a train to Detroit where Vito's brother Giuseppe had been dropped off by their father, Francesco, in 1907 at the age of 15. Giuseppe was operating a produce business with his uncles. Four months after Vito and Provvidenza arrived, their first child, Francesco, was born and was baptized at Holy Family. Vito and Provvidenza were both members of the Madonna delle Grazie Society, and Provvidenza, who outlived her husband by almost 50 years, was a member of the church for 70 years. Pictured from left to right are Provvidenza, Serafina, Frances, Frank, Joseph, and Vito. (Provvidenza [Vitale] Badalamenti.)

Joseph Zerilli celebrates 50 years of marriage with his wife and sisters. All of the Zerilli siblings have a bond to Holy Family. Pictured from left to right are Rosalia Zerilli, who married Vito Tocco; Joseph Zerilli's wife, Josephine Finazzo; Grace Zerilli, who married Russell Cutino; Petrina Zerilli, who married Peter Corrado; and Serafina Zerilli, who married Angelo Gianoso. (Jack Tocco.)

Fr. Joe Muzzin, Anthony D'Anna, and Fr. Noel Patacconi are pictured in front of the Ford Rotunda building. D'Anna was a great friend to the Benedictine fathers, ensuring they had everything they needed. He served his country by selling war bonds and raised $16 million to build the USS Cosselin. D'Anna was a powerful man who supported his church and the Italian community in myriad ways. (Holy Family.)

From left to right, Anthony D'Anna, unidentified, Bill D'Anna, and Fr. Benedict Ferretti are pictured here in front of Anthony's Ford agency in Wyandotte. Joe Zerilli, parish council president for many years, was in charge of the annual Italian feast at the church each year along with Vito Tocco and Anthony D'Anna. As the event served as the major annual fund-raising effort, in alternating years, each man donated a luxury vehicle for raffle since they all owned a dealership. D'Anna was a Ford man, and Zerilli and Tocco represented General Motors. (Joseph D'Anna.)

John Tocco is pictured here on his 50th anniversary with his wife, Mildred, at Holy Family in 1992. Born in 1919, Tocco took most of his sacraments at Holy Family and was a faithful parishioner, maintaining and caring for the church throughout his life. (Johnnie Woolsey.)

Mario and Nancy Viviani have been loyal parish members for more than 50 years, and they raised all of their children and grandchildren in the church. The Vivianis have owned and operated Michigan Artistic Creations for just as long. An artist, Mario has been responsible for the statues in many churches and repairs statuary as well. (Author's collection.)

The Donofrio family has been among the most loyal and generous parishioners of Holy Family since the closing of Santa Maria Church in 1973. The family is pictured here in 1998 at the confirmations of Nino and Angelo. From left to right are Kim Tene, Graziella, Tony, Joe, Andrew (Sonny), and Louise Donofrio. (Joe Donofrio.)

It was often the custom among Sicilians to have an altar or shrine to the holy family in their homes, along with statues of their favorite saints. Antoinette Viviano and Nick Moceri were photographed in their home in the 1930s. (Rosary Amore.)

All three Maniaci girls were baptized at Holy Family. Josephine, Angie, and Ida Maniaci, all dressed in black, are pictured here with the DiMaggio sisters, Rose and Felicia, on the occasion of an engagement party for Angie Maniaci and Sam DiMaggio. The Maniaci girls were in mourning for their mother, Fara. To mourn a death in the family, it was tradition among most Sicilians to wear black for one year, no matter the occasion. (Rose Patchett.)

The Parisi eight are pictured from left to right: Augustine, born 1914, married Lawrence Leto; Providentia, born 1910, married Joseph Vitale; Grace, born 1905, married Vincent Capizzo; Frances, born 1899, married Michael Brigglio; their mother Rosina Parisi; Josephine, born 1903, married Joseph Giorlando; Lena, born 1907, married Matt Ciaramitaro; Rose, born 1912, married Anthony Cilluffo; and Sara, born 1916, married Anthony Leto. The Parisi girls remained loyal to their church. Augustine, age 93, Pearl, age 98, and Lena, age 100, all died in 2007. (Rose Marie Fessler.)

Patrick and Frances Topolewski will always be remembered as two of Holy Family's most generous benefactors. Patrick belonged to the Ushers Club for many years, and Frances was a schoolteacher and also taught catechism. Among their last gifts to the church were a baby grand piano and statue of St. Patrick. (Holy Family.)

After Fr. Benedict Ferretti was made superior of the Holy Face Monastery, Holy Family parishioners and friends of the pastor took an annual bus trip to New Jersey to visit him. Father Ferretti was the longest serving and most beloved priest and administrator of Holy Family Parish. This photograph was taken in the 1970s. (Carl and Eleanora Bommarito.)

Fr. Benedict Ferretti, O.S.B., became superior of the Holy Face Monastery in Clifton, New Jersey. Pictured here on September 25, 1978, are Fr. Benedict Feretti, Rosina Bommarito, her daughter-in-law Eleanora (Imbrunnone), and son Carl Bommarito. On this day they donated this statue of Jesus to the Benedictine monastery. The Bommarito family donated money to numerous projects around the church over the years, such as a stained-glass window and a mural. They also donated countless hours of time to their church and belonged to many organizations such as the Madonna delle Grazie, Altars Society, Ushers Club, Parish Council, Post 570, and Holy Face Society. Rosina lived to be 101. Carl and Eleanora were both baptized at Holy Family. (Carl and Eleanora Bommarito.)

Dino Valle, multitalented member of the Italian community and inspirational voice of Holy Family, Verdi Opera, and Michigan Catholic Radio, is pictured here to the right as master of ceremonies at the 2007 Italian Festival at Freedom Hill. To the left is Dr. Carlo Romeo of the Italian consulate. (Author's collection.)

Joe and Josephine DeMaria are two lifelong members who continue the work begun by their parents. They have spent countless hours of their time to Holy Family not only at mass, but by maintaining and organizing many church events. They are true pillars of strength. (Author's collection.)

This handsome couple is Joseph Amicangelo and his wife, Rose. Joe came to the United States in 1939 from the small town of Pacentro in the province of Aquila in Italy. He married Rose, and they had four beautiful daughters. They have been faithful parishioners for over 50 years. Their presence at Holy Family always brings a smile to others. (Joseph and Rose Amicangelo.)

Andrea Pacitto was scheduled to come to the United States in 1956 on the S.S. *Andrea Doria*. Going against his father's plans, his life was spared. Instead he came shortly after on the *Leonardo di Vinci*. He married a girl, Antoniatta, from his hometown of Valleluce in Italy. Andrea and Antoniatta first came to Holy Family for a midnight mass. He was later asked to join the choir. He has been singing and singing since the age of three, and even though he and his wife have only been parishioners the last decade, they have added an extra grace and beauty to the choir. This photograph is on a return trip to Italy on the *Leonardo di Vinci* with his wife and daughter Maria. (Andrea and Antoniatta Pacitto.)

Many different altar boys have served Holy Family Church over the years. Pictured from left to right are John Oliver, Keith Morrone, David Lanfear, Mario Viviani, and Mark Lanfear. (Keith Morrone.)

In keeping with tradition, Holy Family uses only male altar servers. The servers respond in Latin prayer during mass. They assist the priest and wear the traditional vestments, some almost as old as the church. From left to right are John Pearson, Dr. Anthony Potts, Marcelo Alvarado, Antonio Morrone, Fr. Lawrence Fares, and Keith Morrone. (Author's collection.)

The Holy Family altar boys and their families enjoyed a day at the ball game. Pictured here are Keith and Nicole Morrone, Bonnie and Leo Leone, Jeanette Morrone, Domenick Richardson, Antonio Morrone, and Victoria, Salome, Kathy, Maria, and Marcelo Alvarado. (Author's collection.)

Joseph Donofrio was the confidant and friend of both Fr. Noel Patacconi and Fr. John Stopponi. After several break-ins at the church, Donofrio installed a sophisticated alarm system. He was even able to secure a nighttime police patrol for the church. Joe Donofrio and Kim Tene are pictured here. (Author's collection.)

Katherine Pearson was photographed at the May 2007 crowning of the Blessed Mother, continuing in a 99-year-old tradition of the parish. The Blessed Mother is honored the first Sunday of May each year with a prayer, a procession, singing, and the crowning. (Author's collection.)

The newest statue and centerpiece of the courtyard was donated and erected in 2002 by Andrea and Nina Biondo, Giuseppe and Caterina Biondo, Michele and Maria Biundo, and Girolamo and Rose Mary Vitale. Pictured from left to right are Katherine Pearson, Keith Moronne, Madeline and Samantha Dunlap, Antonio Morrone, Domenick Richardson, Leo Leone, Danielle McDonald, Marcelo Alvarado, Nicolas Delgato, and John Pearson. (Author's collection.)

Leo Leone and Madeline Dunlap, both baptized at Holy Family Church, are standing in front of Madonna del Ponte. They are the youngest weekly parishioners, and by God's good grace the future of the parish. *Cent'anni di piu'!* (Author's collection.)

Visit us at
arcadiapublishing.com